Scholastic World Cultures

SOUTHEAST ASIA

by *Matthew Mestrovic, Ph.D.*

Third Edition

Consultant

LAURISTON SHARP, Ph.D.
Goldwin Smith Professor of Anthropology and Asian Studies
Cornell University

Readability Consultant
LAWRENCE B. CHARRY, Ed.D.

SCHOLASTIC INC.

Titles in This Series
CANADA
CHINA
GREAT BRITAIN
THE INDIAN SUBCONTINENT
JAPAN
LATIN AMERICA
MEXICO
THE MIDDLE EAST
SOUTHEAST ASIA
THE SOVIET UNION AND EASTERN EUROPE
TROPICAL AND SOUTHERN AFRICA
WESTERN EUROPE

ISBN 0-590-34785-3

Matthew Mestrovic is Associate Professor of History and Political Science at Fairleigh Dickinson University. He is a former associate editor of Scholastic Magazines and a former contributing editor of *Time Magazine*. He has contributed articles to many magazines, including *Commonweal, America,* and *Dun's Review.*

Editorial Director for WORLD CULTURES: *Carolyn Jackson*
Contributing Editors: Eleanor Angeles, William Johnson
Assistant Editor: Elise Bauman
Teaching Guide Editor: Frances Plotkin

Art Director and Designer: Irmgard Lochner
Art Assistant: Wilhelmina Reyinga
Photo Editor: Elnora Bode

COVER: "Thailand is a photographers paradise—a splash of bright and cheerful colors...a land dotted with temples, whose red-tiled roofs and golden spires sparkle in the tropical sun. Almost everywhere, the orange robes of Buddhist monks add to the dazzling effect."
—Chapter 2

SOUTHEAST
ASIA

Table of Contents

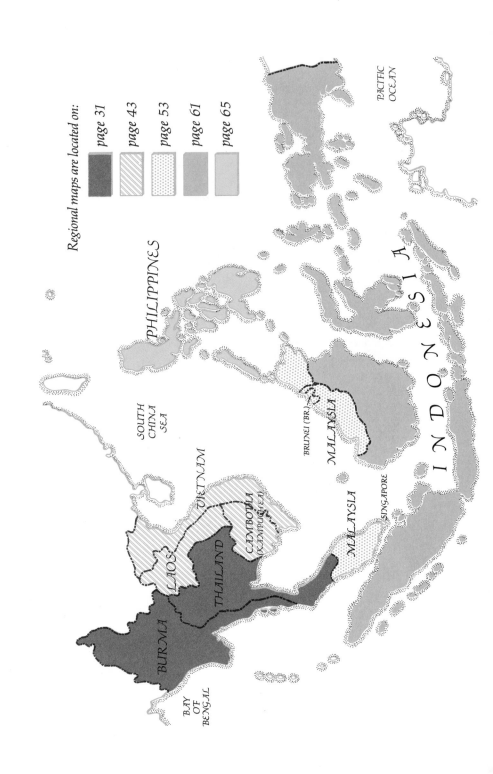

Regional maps are located on:

page 31
page 43
page 53
page 61
page 65

PACIFIC OCEAN

PHILIPPINES

SOUTH CHINA SEA

VIETNAM

LAOS

BURMA

THAILAND

CAMBODIA (KAMPUCHEA)

BAY OF BENGAL

BRUNEI (BR.)

MALAYSIA

MALAYSIA

SINGAPORE

INDONESIA

⋙ When the monsoon is spent
in the fields extensively
the thriving rice
is diffused with gold
yellow and brilliant.

Should the pretty one
eager to know
question me whether
I have bullion gold
I should show her
this golden rice.

UNKNOWN BURMESE POET

PROLOGUE

FIRST
ENCOUNTER

ONE OF THE WORLD'S best-loved adventure stories tells of an Arab named Sinbad the Sailor. This legendary man of the sea journeyed to the distant Spice

Islands — islands rich in pepper, cinnamon, and other spices. Some of these islands were governed by all-powerful kings who lived in palaces glittering with rubies and diamonds.

Fantastic? Yes. But partly true.

The Sinbad stories are based on the real adventures of Arab sailors and merchants who did visit the Spice Islands centuries ago. They returned telling tales of wild adventures and of riches beyond compare.

Today these Spice Islands are part of the East Indies. Four nations—Indonesia,* the Philippines,* Brunei,* and part of Malaysia*—now make up most of the islands in the East Indies. They, in turn, are part of a larger region that also includes the five Asian countries of Vietnam, Laos,* Cambodia (also called Kampuchea), Burma, and Thailand.*

To Australians, who live slightly to the south, the area is known as "the Near North." By the people of the Indian subcontinent, it is called "Further China." But to most other people today, this region of soaring mountains and roaring rivers, of broad valleys and lush jungles, is known as Southeast Asia.

Southeast Asia caught the world's attention as war and revolution swept the area during the past three decades. But long before the advent of violence in the region, Southeast Asia commanded a unique, important place in the world. Few other areas contain such a rich blend of peoples, customs, and beliefs. Here four of the world's greatest cultures—Chinese, Indian, Moslem, and European—have made their impact on the area's way of life. Here more religions live side-by-side and more important languages are spoken than in almost any other region in the world.

---

*See Pronunciation Guide.

Each country of Southeast Asia has its own mixture of peoples. Some people are related in language and custom, some are not. The result is a bewildering variety of peoples and cultures.

Take Burma, for example. The gentle, easy-going Burmans make up almost three-fourths (72%) of the country's population of 37 million. But there are also Shans* in their baggy pants and turbans. There are warlike Karens,* and Nagas* who live in remote areas. And there are other groups as well (see page 29).

The situation is similar in Indonesia. The many people of this sprawling island republic speak more than a hundred languages and dialects and they belong to almost as many different ethnic groups. Indonesia's national motto proclaims "Unity in Diversity." But the country's history, even in recent times, reveals as much diversity as unity.

The result of all this mixing and blending is a region where the contrasts seem endless. In addition, European culture has also left a deep imprint on its ways of life. Perhaps what most impresses the Western visitor to Southeast Asia now, in fact, is the curious blend of old and new. The contrast is probably most jarring between the great cities — Jakarta* in Indonesia, Bangkok* in Thailand, Ho Chi Minh* City in Vietnam — and the countryside, where eight out of every 10 people still live.

For example, Jakarta, Indonesia's capital, is a thriving city of almost eight million people, with high-rise buildings and car-clogged streets. Jets take off from the city's modern airport — and within minutes fly over mountains where nearly naked tribesmen hunt with poison darts.

Some places in Southeast Asia are as new as tomorrow. Most of Southeast Asia was old when recorded time began.

1
NATIONS
AND
CULTURES

Chapter 1

The Land

PERHAPS THE TITLE of this chapter ought to be "The Lands" — in the plural, rather than singular — for Southeast Asia is made up not of one land, but of many. The 10 countries of Southeast Asia are located on a variety of terrains. They range from highlands to lowlands, from jungle-covered mountains and fertile deltas to desert (and deserted) islands.

Curving down and around like a giant crescent, Southeast Asia points one end upward into China and the other end outward into the South Pacific (see map, page 6). The crescent stretches east to west for 4,000 miles, which is about the distance between Chicago and Honolulu, and from north to south about 2,200 miles, about the distance between Dallas and Juneau,* Alaska. So Southeast Asia spreads out over a great deal of territory. But much of that area is water. The land area alone is only about one half the size of the United States.

The 10 countries of Southeast Asia fall into two clear geographic regions. One group is on the southeastern-most tip of the Asian mainland that juts into the South China Sea. In this group are Burma, Thailand, Laos, Cambodia, and Vietnam. The other group is made up of two sprawling island nations—Indonesia with 13,677 islands and islets, and the Philippines, with its 7,100 islands and islets. One country, Malaysia, is in both groups. Part of Malaysia is on the edge of the mainland. The other part is on the huge island of Borneo, which Malaysia shares with Indonesia and newly independent Brunei.* Finally, there is the small island nation of Singapore,* which lies just off the tip of the Asian mainland group.

The two regions of Southeast Asia are vastly different in geography. On the mainland, mountain chains run north and south, dividing the region into broad river valleys. Here the land varies swiftly within just a few miles. There are forest-covered highlands. There are vast jungles and swamps. There are coastal plains and watery deltas good for rice-growing, and inland plateaus producing a wide variety of crops.

Most of the people who live in mainland Southeast Asia live in the fertile valleys near the broad rivers. As the mountains tend to block movement *between* different valleys, most travel on the mainland takes place up and down the river valleys.

The rivers themselves are the main highways of travel and trade (*see* page 131). Some rise in or near the mountains of Tibet and flow south to the Bay of Bengal and the South China Sea. As the rivers move south, they carry rich soil washed down from the mountains and valleys by the heavy rains. When this soil reaches the mouths of the rivers, it spreads out to form triangle-shaped areas called deltas. The deltas grow so big, in fact, that they must be cut through

*Southeast Asia's tropical climate wraps the area
in a cloak of green. Most of the region gets
more than 60 inches of rain a year. In some lands
the rain comes mainly in the monsoon season.
But in Malaysia (above) it comes all year long.*

with dredges every so often. This is needed to let
oceangoing ships reach the port cities near the river
mouths.

Perhaps the most surprising thing about the island
region of Southeast Asia, the other region, is its rich
variety. Hardly any two of the 20,000 islands and islets
which make up Indonesia and the Philippines are alike.
Some are so barren and rocky that no human lives on

them. Others, like the island of Java* in Indonesia, are so rich and pleasant that they are among the most densely populated places on the face of the earth. With more than 167 million people, Indonesia ranks as the world's fifth-largest country. But more than half of that population is crowded onto the island of Java.

Many of the islands in both the Philippines and Indonesia are unfit for the kind of rice-growing culture that supports most Southeast Asians. Some islands are too dry. Others are too wet and swampy — an unhealthy environment for humans. Still others are largely made up of volcanoes, some of which have a nasty habit of erupting from time to time.

But those who live near volcanoes also find that there are some benefits from doing so. Volcanic ash from eruptions coats the farmlands. This ash has organic materials which enrich the soil and make for abundant crops.

It's hot in most of Southeast Asia, and often muggy. That's because it is close to the Equator, close to the sea, and in the monsoon* belt as well. The monsoon is a strong wind and a heavy rain that come for several months at the same time each year. In summer the land heats up, and the wind and rain rush in from the cooler sea. In winter the land cools down and sends the wind back over the warmer sea. The summer monsoon hits much of mainland Southeast Asia. However, the winter monsoon strikes the east coasts of Borneo and the Philippines and the Vietnam coastline as well. Much of Indonesia, on the other hand, has no real monsoon season. In many areas of Indonesia, it rains just about every day, winter or summer.

This combination of heat and humidity produces a lush growth of tropical trees and wild flowers. In the

16

POPULATION DISTRIBUTION

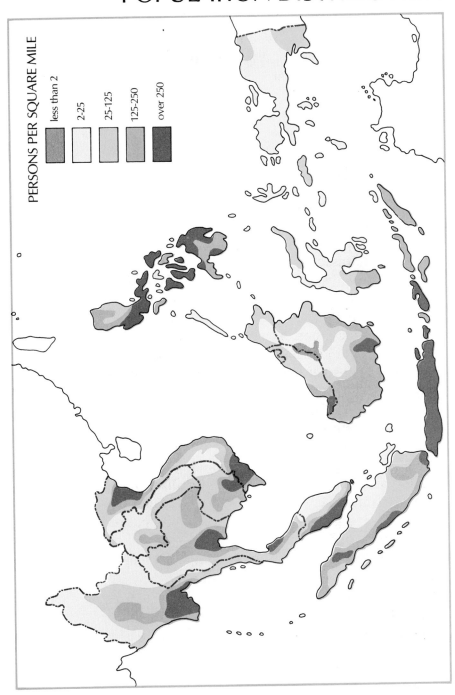

PERSONS PER SQUARE MILE

less than 2
2-25
25-125
125-250
over 250

rain forests the trees soar to dizzying heights. In the open fields, thousands of different flowers bloom in a giant crazy-quilt of colors.

Elsewhere there are dozens of kinds of fruit ready for picking. The papaya is a red, juicy fruit that tastes a little like a very ripe peach. Another fruit, the breadfruit, looks and feels like fresh bread when baked, but with a taste all its own. But watch out for the durian!* Although it tastes good, it has a foul smell. If you can hold your nose while eating it, you'll like it.

Farms cover about a fifth of the land in Southeast Asia. The deltas, constantly enriched by new soil deposits, are always fertile. So are the lands at the feet of volcanoes which have benefited from the rich volcanic ash. But the remainder of the land is not especially good for crops. True, it can grow a splendid show of trees and wild flowers. But ask the land to grow food crops year after year, and it does less well with each new planting.

In part, this is because many Southeast Asian farmers use "slash-and-burn" methods of farming. A farmer moves into a forested site; cuts down the trees, letting them lie where they fall; and sets fire to the whole area. The ashes make good fertilizer, and the farmer plants his crop in the burned-over soil. "Slash-and-burn" is a good, quick way to get the land ready for planting.

But the ashes are effective for only a few seasons. Gradually the land loses its fertility. Without trees, the topsoil quickly washes away in the heavy rains. Then the farmer leaves his unproductive field, finds another forested site, and goes through the same process again.

Southeast Asian farmers raise a variety of crops depending on the climate and location, but the big-

LAND USE

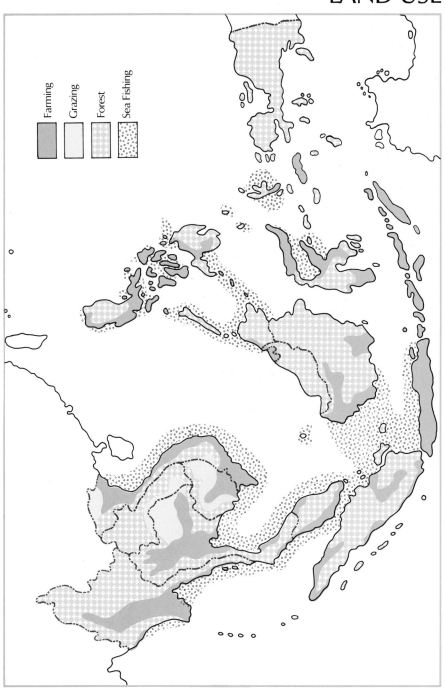

Farming

Grazing

Forest

Sea Fishing

gest and most important crop is rice. It is grown throughout the area much as it was a thousand years ago. Perhaps the most common sight for anyone who travels through the region is that of the farmer bent in the field, knee-deep in water, planting the little green stalks. Nearby a water buffalo toils just as patiently at the task of plowing the land.

Rice is central to the life-styles of many Southeast Asians. When the monsoon comes and the rains begin, the fields and hillsides are alive with movement and farmers. People toil from dawn to dusk preparing the soil and planting their crops. Once the rains are over and the harvest is in, life is taken at ease — until the next planting cycle gets under way.

Obviously, a lot depends on the coming of the monsoons. If the monsoon is late or if the rains are light, the lives and livelihoods of millions of people are placed in the balance. On the other hand, too much of a monsoon is not good either. Cyclones can develop, bringing torrential rains and high winds that whip through the flimsy dwellings of the poor people.

For all its charm and beauty, then, Southeast Asia has its share of natural hazards. Its people know that nature can bring them prosperity — and can also take it away.

The Mekong River makes a wide U-turn at the Thai-Laotian border as it pushes smoothly and slowly toward the sea.

THE MEKONG: RICE-GIVING RIVER

IN THE SPRING of each year, the sun begins beating down with renewed strength. Then, some of the snow on the slopes of the Himalaya* Mountains melts into crystal-clear streams which glide down toward the south and east. The waters flow out of Tibet and down through the valleys of southern China, gathering momentum with each mile. Soon the waters become a torrential river showing its force in white water, rapids, and waterfalls. Where the river forms the boundary between Burma and Laos, and between Laos and Thailand, it is then deemed worthy of the name of a great river: the Mekong.*

Fed by the monsoon rains, the Mekong floods the plains of central Laos, preparing the earth for rich rice harvests. By the time the Mekong reaches the Laotian capital of Vientiane,* it is no longer clear and sparkling but big, wide, and mud-brown. Since this part of Laos is virtually roadless, the Mekong is the main route of transportation. Most of the area's population lives near it.

Further down-river, the Mekong enters the flat Cambodian plain. At Cambodia's capital, Phnom Penh,* the Mekong intersects with another river, the Tonle Sap.* At this point, the waters of the two rivers flow into small tributaries and filter down through the swampy delta of Vietnam into the South China Sea.

In midsummer, when the monsoon rains come down in torrents and the Tibetan snows melt rapidly, there is more water than these tributary streams can absorb. Then a strange phenomenon occurs. The waters of the Mekong rush down with such force that they push the Tonle Sap upstream, forcing it to reverse its current. The Tonle Sap backs up in a great shallow lake which overflows and floods 4,000 square miles of soil.

In the fall, the Himalayan thaw ends, and the snows no longer melt. The monsoon rains end too. The river, no longer swollen, returns to normal. The Tonle Sap again reverses direction and flows downstream once more. The flood subsides from the plain, leaving behind a layer of fertile soil just right for the rice crop. As the water level recedes, millions of fish are trapped in shallow pools and delivered practically into the baskets of the fishermen.

To give thanks for the waters' gifts, the people who live in the basin of the Mekong stage festivals. Laotians launch miniature boats made of palm leaves and decorated with candles which light up the Mekong with flickering reflections. In Cambodia, the annual Water Festival lasts three days and three nights. Almost every village along the river sends a team to the *pirogue*,* or canoe, races held at Phnom Penh near the point where

Mekong River Development Project

CHINA

CHINA

BURMA

LAOS
● Luang Prabang
■ UPPER LUANG PRABANG

■■ LOWER LUANG PRABANG

VIETNAM
● Vientiane
PA MONG   THAKHEK ■

Mekong River

THAILAND
KHEMARAT

BURMA

CAMBODIA
(KAMPUCHEA)   ■ KHONE FALLS

■ SAMBOR

TONLE SAP ■
Phnom Penh ●

● Ho Chi Minh City

SOUTH
CHINA
SEA

Feet above sea level

UPPER LUANG PRABANG
LOWER LUANG PRABANG
PA MONG
THAKHEK
KHEMARAT
KHONE FALLS
TONLE SAP   SAMBOR

1000
800
600
400
200
0

0   200   400   600   800   1000   1200   1400
Miles from Mekong River mouth

23

the Mekong meets the Tonle Sap. The rowers are costumed in silk, and the pirogues are decorated in the special colors of their villages. At night, elaborate floats lit with colored electric lights entertain the people and pay homage to the spirit of the river.

Colorful as these festivals are, the nations of the Mekong basin look forward to the day when they are less dependent on the whims of season and weather. Under the sponsorship of the United Nations, these countries are working out a joint system of dams and reservoirs.

This system goes by the name of the Mekong River Development Project. Under present plans, the project is slated to consist of eight main dams. These dams will be constructed along the river as it flows from the northern mountains to the southern sea. They will be spotted all the way from Luang Prabang* in Laos to the Tonle Sap in Cambodia (see map, page 23).

When completed, these dams will serve three purposes. First, they will control the flow of the river. Second, they will provide water for irrigating the region's farmland. Third, they will harness electricity for power. The planners hope that the program, when completed, will transform the mighty 2,500 mile-long Mekong River from an uncertain master to a faithful servant of the people of the river basin.

Double-check

Review

1. Why could the title of this chapter be "The Lands" instead of "The Land"?

2. What is the world's fifth-largest country?

3. What is the most important crop in Southeast Asia?

4. By the time the Mekong River reaches Vientiane, how does it look?

5. What three purposes are served by the main dams on the Mekong River?

Discussion

1. This chapter describes some ways that land and climate help shape the lives of people in Southeast Asia. *Where* people live often influences *how* they live. Think of ways this is true for *your* community. Then compare your community with the information about Southeast Asia in the chapter.

2. Rivers play extremely important roles in Southeast Asia. How many different roles do they seem to play? How do these roles compare with the ways rivers are used in the United States?

3. What impressions do you have of Southeast Asia as you begin this book? What are the main sources of these impressions? What questions would you like to have answered about Southeast Asia?

Activities

1. A committee of students might be formed to prepare a large wall map of Southeast Asia for use with this and future chapters. They could use the map on page 6 as a guide and then add information to it from other maps, including others in this book.

2. Thirteen words in Chapter 1 are starred (*). This indicates that these words are in the Pronunciation Guide at the back of the book. A committee of students might assume primary responsibility for teaching fellow students how to pronounce these words. They could do this, in advance, for all future chapters.

3. The photo essays near the center of this book show the diversity of the land, people, economy, and culture of Southeast Asia. You might look at these photos now and mark on a map the places they show.

Skills

POPULATION OF SOUTHEAST ASIAN COUNTRIES

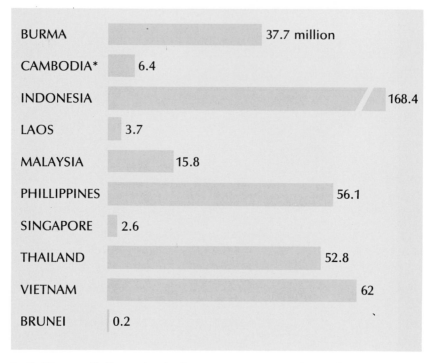

BURMA — 37.7 million
CAMBODIA* — 6.4
INDONESIA — 168.4
LAOS — 3.7
MALAYSIA — 15.8
PHILLIPPINES — 56.1
SINGAPORE — 2.6
THAILAND — 52.8
VIETNAM — 62
BRUNEI — 0.2

*called Democratic Kampuchea by the source. Source: *Population Reference Bureau,1986*

Use the bar graph above and information in Chapter 1 to answer the following questions.

1. This graph shows the population of how many countries?
(a) one   (b) 10   (c) two

2. For what year are these numbers valid?
(a) 1986   (b) 1979   (c) 1976

3. Which country has the smallest population?
(a) Indonesia   (b) Singapore   (c) Brunei

4. Where does most of the information in this graph come from?
(a) Cambodia's government   (b) United Nations
(c) Population Reference Bureau

5. The island just off the tip of the Asian mainland has about how many people?
(a) 62 millin   (b) 2.6 million   (c) 52.8 million

Chapter 2

Burma and Thailand: The Gentle Life in the Golden Land

DRENCHED WITH PERSPIRATION, an exhausted group of Americans hacked their way through the tangled, malaria-ridden jungles of northern Burma in the mid-1940's. In just a few months, these men and an army of Chinese and Burmese laborers carved out a 478-mile highway. This was an extension of the Burma Road, and it played a key role in World War II. Over it, trucks carried supplies to China, then fighting for its life against the Japanese.

The Americans could hardly be blamed if they found Burma far from appealing. But they saw only one side of the country. Fanning out to the south of the rugged mountains is another Burma — a region of gently rolling plains, green rice fields, and low-lying hills.

27

This land basks in a warm tropical sun, which makes the slender spires of the many Buddhist* temples shimmer like golden needles. The quiet beauty of the countryside, the shining buildings, and the bright orange robes of the Buddhist monks have given Burma the nickname "the Golden Land."

The Burmese too seem to feel that their land is something special. Unlike their neighbors, the Thais, the Burmese have never shown any great eagerness to travel abroad or to adopt foreign ways or fads. Even in Burma's cities, which might be expected to be more open to outside ways, a Burmese businessman is more likely to wear a *longyi*,* a length of cloth draped from the waist, than a business suit.

If there is one thing most Burmese take seriously it is religion. Most Burmese are devout Buddhists. A look at Rangoon,* Burma's capital, bears this out. Rangoon is filled with countless Buddhist shrines, including the magnificent Shwe Dagon* pagoda. Its gold-leafed, jewel-studded spire towers over the city.

The Burmese are not one people, but many. They come from about 50 different groups and subgroups and speak more than 100 different languages and dialects. All the varied people who are citizens of Burma are called *Burmese.*

But almost three-fourths of the Burmese are Burmans, a group which long ago migrated south from Central Asia. Most Burmans live in the central lowlands of Burma. Around them live a number of other Burmese groups. There are Shans on the eastern plateau, Kachins in the north near the Chinese border, and Karens scattered throughout the south. There are also about a

On his weekly trip to market, a Shan villager tests tea in a city square in Burma. How does his shopping tour differ from one in the U.S.?

million Indians and Chinese, late arrivals on the Burmese scene.

Many of these minority peoples have never fully accepted Burman domination of the country. In fact, differences among the peoples of Burma have been one of the major themes of recorded Burmese history. The times when strong leadership has been able to unite these diverse peoples can be counted on the fingers of one hand.

It happened first in 1044, when King Anawhrata* unified the tribes which had migrated into Burma from China and Tibet several centuries earlier. He founded a kingdom at Pagan,* a mighty capital with beautiful gold-covered Buddhist pagodas and glittering palaces. In the 13th century, however, the days of glory came to a sad end when Mongol armies from the north swept in and sacked Pagan.

Not until the 16th century was Burma again united. The man who then put it all together was Bayinnaung,* one of Burma's most powerful rulers. During his rule he conquered all of what is today Thailand and parts of Laos. But after his death, Burmese power again declined.

Burma was united for the third time in the 18th century. To celebrate the achievement, the Burmese ruler founded a new city. He optimistically called it Rangoon — meaning "the end of strife."

It was not the end of strife, however. Trouble soon came from a new corner. Britain, which had taken over India, did the same to Burma. The British turned Burma into the world's leading rice exporter. They built railways, roads, and telegraph lines.

The British also built schools, hospitals — and jails. Over the years, these jails housed many young Burmese who led strikes and protests against British rule.

In 1941, at the same time that Japan attacked Pearl Harbor, it also invaded Burma. U.S. and British forces retook the country in 1945. Three years later Burma won independence from Britain and became a republic.

Since then, Burma has had all the satisfactions — and many of the troubles — of a newly independent nation. But unlike many newly independent nations, Burma has a lot going for it.

Crops grow well in Burma because of the easy availability of water. The mighty, broad Irrawaddy* and Salween* rivers run the length of the land and spill into the neighboring rice fields. The heavy monsoon rains, which arrive in May and stay until October, also irrigate the fertile soil.

To outsiders, life in Burma seems relaxed and easygoing. Most Burmese are farmers who earn little money but still survive with little trouble on the food they grow themselves.

☆ ☆ ☆ ☆ ☆ ☆ ☆ ☆ ☆

Thailand is a photographer's paradise — a splash of bright and cheerful colors. It is a land dotted with temples, whose red-tiled roofs and golden spires sparkle in the tropical sun. Almost everywhere, the orange robes of Buddhist monks add to the dazzling effect.

The Thais occupy a country about three quarters the size of Texas. Thailand is shaped roughly like the head of an elephant, which is appropriate because the elephant has long been a national symbol. On the map the elephant's forehead is the northern region, a mountainous area of heavy teak forests. The trunk twists down the narrow Malay Peninsula, an area of sparkling beaches, hills, and tropical forests.

Glittering statue of a demon keeps vigil outside the Temple of the Emerald Buddha on the grounds of the Royal Palace in Bangkok.

Near the elephant's "mouth" is a fertile central plain, watered by a river called Mae Nam Chao Phraya* ("Mother of Waters Most Noble") or, more simply, the Chao Phraya. The river rises in the jungle-covered mountains of the north; drops through wild, beautiful gorges; and rolls past the city of Bangkok to the Gulf of Siam.* A large, dry plateau covers the elephant's "ear" to the east.

In Thailand, farmers can expect rain from May to November, and a dry season for the rest of the year. During the dry season, the fields may be parched and cracked. But there is water aplenty during the rainy season, enabling the Thai farmer to produce huge quantities of rice. This is one reason why Thailand is one of the world's leading exporters of rice. Thai rice helps feed hungry stomachs throughout Southeast Asia.

Thai farmers are fortunate for reasons other than their large crop yields. They have no "landlord problem," for most of them own the land they till.

Other products of Thailand's soil are rubber — grown mainly in the south — and teak. One of the hardest woods in the world, teak is widely used in shipbuilding. In the huge forests which cover three fifths of Thailand, lumberjacks fell the teak trees. Trained elephants then drag the logs to rivers, where the wood is floated downstream to sawmills.

Bangkok has often been called the "Venice of the Orient" because of its network of *klongs*,* or canals (see page 84). Above the canals, houses rise on stilts like long-legged water spiders. The waterways are crowded with houseboats and "floating markets" — boats loaded with vegetables, fruits, charcoal, and other goods for sale.

The great majority of Thailand's inhabitants are Thais, a people similar to Burmans and Laotians. Three thousand years ago, the ancestors of the present Thai people lived in South China. Under constant pressure from the Chinese, the Thais began moving southward. They finally arrived in present-day Thailand, naming their new home Muang Thai* — "Land of the Free."

About A.D. 1350, the Thais founded a powerful kingdom at Ayutthaya,* near Bangkok. This kingdom was still flourishing in 1511, when the Portuguese, the first European visitors, arrived in Thailand.

After the Portuguese came Spanish, Dutch, British, and French traders. Thailand, or Siam as it was known to Europeans at that time, established close contacts with these newcomers. It permitted them to live at Ayutthaya and trade there.

But many Siamese nobles became uneasy at the power of the Europeans. Alarmed, they rose in revolt, kicked out all foreigners, and isolated themselves from the Western world.

For the next hundred years, the Siamese were almost constantly at war with neighboring Burma. The Burmese managed to conquer the Thais in the late 18th century. But the Thais soon rallied and drove the Burmese out of their country.

By the middle of the 19th century, Europeans were again threatening Siam. The British had taken Malaya to the south and were busy carving up Burma to the west. In the north and east, France had begun to gobble up the states which were to become the French colonies of Indochina.

Siam escaped the fate of its neighbors for two reasons. First, the British and French wanted a neutral "buffer state" between their colonies in Southeast Asia. Second, Siam had the good fortune to be ruled by some remarkable kings.

One of them was Mongkut,* who became king in

35

1851. He is known to the West chiefly as the shirtless, hairless ruler in the movie musical *The King and I.* The musical was based on the book *Anna and the King of Siam* by Margaret Landon.

Mongkut was a very different person from the man portrayed in the musical and the book. He was a scholar who had spent 27 years as a Buddhist monk before gaining the throne. He was not hairless when he was king; he had shaved his head only while he had been a monk.

Mongkut decided that Siam must learn about Western science and technology in order to avoid becoming a colony. He studied English and Latin. He corresponded with Abraham Lincoln and Britain's Queen Victoria. By skillfully playing off Britain against France, he and his son were able to preserve Siam's independence.

The kings of Siam lost most of their power in 1932. An army group seized control and turned Siam into a constitutional monarchy on the pattern of Britain. In the years since then, control of the Thai government has switched back and forth between military and civilian leaders.

Thailand, then, is the only country in Southeast Asia which has never been a colony of a European nation. Perhaps that explains why Western visitors are usually impressed by the easygoing friendliness of the Thais. Since the Thais have never been subject to European rule, they seem to have little antagonism toward Europeans.

The Buddhist religion — which teaches tolerance, patience, and goodwill — has also affected the character of the Thai people. The Thais have a saying, *mai pen arai.* * It roughly means: "Don't worry about it; it doesn't mean anything." This saying has come in handy in good times and bad.

Double-check

Review

1. What has given Burma the nickname "the Golden Land"?

2. How many different groups and subgroups do the Burmese people come from?

3. What country is one of the world's leading exporters of rice?

4. Why has Bangkok often been called the "Venice of the Orient"?

5. When was Thailand a colony of a European nation?

Discussion

1. This chapter points out that the Burmese are not eager to travel abroad or to adopt "foreign ways or fads." What long-term effects could such isolationism have on a nation and its people? Do you think many Americans would like to travel abroad? Are Americans generally open to fads from foreign countries? Give examples to support your answers.

2. Thailand was never under European rule. How might this have been the result of King Mongkut's willingness to learn Western ways? Do you think he could have kept Siam independent without knowing his "enemies"? Why, or why not?

3. Thailand was a neutral buffer state between British and French colonies. Can you name some other countries that have been generally neutral in world affairs? How might such neutrality affect a country? Could, or should, the U.S. try to become neutral toward all other nations of the world? Why, or why not?

Activities

1. Several students might take turns pretending to be the Shan villager buying tea in the photo in this chapter. Other students could role-play the part of the seller, who speaks a different language. They should try to negotiate the purchase of an ounce of tea at a fair price — without using words, either spoken or written.

2. Two small groups of students might research and report on the roles of canals in the cities of Bangkok, Thailand, and Venice, Italy.

3. Some students might read the book *Anna and the King of Siam,* while others read the screenplay for the movie or the script of the play *The King and I.* Afterward the students might compare and contrast the information in each. Then they might listen to the record from the movie and/or the play.

Skills

Use the map and other information in Chapter 2 to answer the following questions.

1. Which two countries are shown in greatest detail on this map?
(a) Burma and China   (b) Burma and Laos   (c) Thailand and Burma

2. The Mekong River forms part of the border between Thailand and which other country?
(a) Burma   (b) Laos   (c) China

3. The Irrawaddy River empties into which body of water?
(a) Bay of Bengal   (b) Andaman Sea   (c) Mekong River

4. The Burma Road crosses the Mekong River in which country?
(a) Burma   (b) China   (c) Laos

5. Which national capital might be said to be near "the elephant's mouth"?
(a) Rangoon   (b) Hanoi   (c) Bangkok

Chapter 3

Vietnam, Laos, and Cambodia: To Bend Without Breaking

BECAUSE OF THEIR POSITION just east of India and just south of China, the three separate countries of Vietnam, Laos, and Cambodia are sometimes known as Indochina. The cultures of all of these countries owe much to China, which at various times during the past 2,000 years has dominated parts of the area.

In the past, the area was also influenced by Hindu cultures which had originated in India. Today, however, the Indian influence is very weak. Still, most of the people of the region follow the Buddhist religion, which originated in India.

But calling the area by the name "Indochina" may give the impression that the area has one culture, one language, one set of values. Nothing could be more wrong. Actually there are many different cultures that mix and merge and conflict in this region.

Sadly, one of the few things that bound the countries of Indochina during the past three decades was violence. These countries found themselves caught up in a larger struggle between powerful nations in a divided world. How this struggle affected day-to-day life is the subject of a later section of this book (see page 197). We are concerned here with the traditional values and cultures of these peoples. For these values and cultures have shown surprising strength that may allow them to endure long after the wars of the past 30 years have become a matter only for history books.

☆ ☆ ☆ ☆ ☆ ☆ ☆ ☆ ☆

Vietnam occupies a territory that has been, throughout history, a crossroads — and sometimes a battlefield — of different cultures. Bordering on China, Vietnam has always been subject to the influences of Chinese civilization and power. In fact, for more than a thousand years, starting in 111 B.C., the Chinese ruled northern Vietnam as a colony.

The Vietnamese are partly the product of these influences. They borrowed ideas and traits from the Chinese, Indians, French, and other groups. Over the centuries, they adapted these ideas and traits to their own use.

The Vietnamese, in contrast to many of their more easygoing neighbors in Southeast Asia, have the reputation of being hard workers. Visitors are usually impressed by the energy and sense of order which is seen almost everywhere.

The most heavily settled areas in Vietnam have been, traditionally, the valley of the Red River in the northern part and the delta of the Mekong River in the southern part.

Slogging through the mud of a flooded rice field, a Vietnamese farmer guides his water buffalo in the annual job of plowing.

Rice, the most important crop, is widely grown in the two river valleys. For this reason, Vietnam is often pictured as two rice baskets carried on a pole. The baskets are the two river valleys, and the pole is the rugged Annamite* chain of mountains which nudges up against the borders of Laos and Cambodia.

Hanoi* and Ho Chi Minh City, the two most populous cities in Vietnam, bear the mark of the French presence. Both are cities with tree-lined boulevards, sidewalk cafes, fountains, and flower markets. Cars, scooters, buses, and other vehicles share the crowded streets. Vietnamese women glide by in their silk *ao dai** dresses, a national costume that enhances their natural gracefulness. People speak in a variety of tongues — English and French as well as Vietnamese.

But there is a different world outside the cities. The smaller towns and villages in Vietnam are really more like agricultural settlements — where the people live, in most respects, like their parents and grandparents before them. As with people all over Southeast Asia, life revolves around the planting and harvesting of rice.

To strangers the Vietnamese often seem shy and reserved. For example, they ordinarily consider such Western expressions of friendship as handshaking and backslapping to be rude. The traditional Vietnamese greeting is a slight bow, hands held before the body with palms curved upward.

By Western standards, the Vietnamese live simply but most of them are not desperately poor. When war was not raging, very few people in Vietnam went hungry. Normally rice was plentiful, as were fish, pineapples, mangoes, and a vast variety of other fruits.

Within their villages and hamlets, most Vietnamese families followed a daily routine typical of a rice-farming society. Peasants, clad in loose-fitting,

pajamalike clothes, and cone-shaped hats, toiled each day in the muddy fields. Often older children pitched in to help with the seeding, transplanting, and harvesting.

At home, the Vietnamese lived according to a strict code of conduct. This code was based partly on the teachings of the ancient Chinese sage, Confucius.* Under it, parents are expected to treat their children with affection, but also with firmness. In return, the children were taught to give complete devotion and respect to their elders.

Respect for authority, social harmony, self-discipline — these were values closely followed in Vietnam. Many of these values have been jolted severely, and some destroyed, by more than 30 years of war.

The Vietnamese like to compare themselves to the bamboo plant. It is a tough plant, but it seldom breaks because it bends with the wind. Similarly, the Vietnamese are hardy people who have often bounced back from past catastrophes.

☆   ☆   ☆   ☆   ☆   ☆   ☆   ☆   ☆

Laotians have a reputation for being a happy, peaceful people. Yet since 1959 they have been short on both happiness and peace. Their country has been torn by political and armed conflict, with family fighting family.

Indeed, Laos was one of the major victims of the turmoil that swept Southeast Asia during the past 30 years (see page 217). But many Laotians maintain what has been their traditional philosophy of life: "Whatever will be, will be." They try to accept what fate brings.

Religion has played a role in molding the easygoing nature of the Laotians. Buddhism teaches toleration, moderation, and a respect for all living things.

At some point in his life, nearly every man or boy in Laos shaves his head, dons orange robes, and serves as a Buddhist monk.

Laos is a land of jungles and mountains, broken by a few plains and high plateaus. Winding along its western border is the broad, fertile valley of the Mekong River.

The valley of the Mekong and its tributary rivers is the richest area of the country. Here are most of the thousands of villages that Laotians usually call home. A typical village is made up of about 200 people, many of whom are related in some way to one another.

Their homes are bamboo, palm-thatched huts, often mounted on stilts several feet off the ground. The stilts are used to keep the huts from being swept away during the May-October rainy season when torrential downpours swell the rivers over their banks. In the dry season, the area under the house serves as a nice, shady spot with lots of fresh air.

Practically all Laotians are farmers and live in villages. Even the two biggest "cities" of Laos — Luang Prabang and Vientiane — are really little more than overgrown villages.

Outside the "cities," communications are unreliable. In fact, just getting around is a problem — and sometimes it is impossible. Most Laotian roads are unpaved and turn into quagmires during the wet season. Automobiles are a rare sight. Almost all are owned by foreigners and top government officials.

Actually, the best form of transport is still walking. For heavy hauling, trained elephants continue to serve Laotians as combination bulldozers and trucks. The faithful, uncomplaining water buffalo remains Laos' answer to modern farm tractors.

A primitive picture? Perhaps by Western standards, but most Laotians don't search after the mate-

✑ Most male Cambodians spent at least part of their lives as Buddhist monks.

rial things that often are equated with "civilization" in the West. Laotians are courteous, modest, and friendly. One enthusiastic foreigner who visited Laos in the 19th century called Laos "a privileged corner where customs retain an exquisite simplicity." To many Laotians, such a description means more than all the goods and conveniences of a modern industrial society.

✿ ✿ ✿ ✿ ✿ ✿ ✿ ✿ ✿

Late each May, crowds of Cambodians would jam into the palace grounds in Phnom Penh to witness an ancient ceremony called "Plowing the Royal Furrow." The ceremony was held just about the time when the monsoon winds announced the beginning of another rainy season. It was a time for Cambodian farmers to begin planting their rice fields.

This is how the ceremony went: Three bowls were placed in the palace courtyard. One was filled with water. Another was filled with rice. The third was left empty. Carefully selected bulls were then led into the courtyard and released.

If the bulls went to the bowl filled with water, rainfall would be abundant. If they went to the bowl of rice, the harvest promised to be good. But if they went to the empty bowl, then, alas, it was a sign of hard times ahead for Cambodia.

These days, the ceremony is tragically outdated. Since the mid-1970's, Cambodians have been the victims of war and famine that have threatened the extinction of the Cambodian nation. Ancient customs and beliefs have been severely tested (see Chapter 19).

For hundreds of years, Buddhist monks led the faithful in religious ceremonies at Angkor,* Cambodia. Nine of every 10 Cambodians were followers of Buddhism, which was the official religion of the nation until 1976.

By the yardsticks used throughout much of the Western world, Cambodia would certainly be classified as a developing nation. Life expectancy is estimated at 43 years. The death rate among the newly born runs as high as 160 per 1,000. More than half the people can neither read nor write.

Yet these statistics do not completely measure the life of a people. For in any discussion of "standards of living" the first step should be to determine whose standard of living is being talked about.

The average Cambodian, for example, probably

did not feel at all deprived before the fighting that shook the country. In peacetime, Cambodians lived in a generous land which, with some hard work, usually provided all the basic needs. "Our bowls are always full" was a popular Cambodian saying.

Most foreigners tend to think of Asian nations in terms of teeming masses. Japan, for example, has some 800 people for each square mile. But Cambodia has a population density of only 100 persons per square mile. This was 120 per square mile before famine and war in the mid-1970's killed millions.

Between 85 and 90 percent of the population are descendants of the Khmers,* a people who founded a powerful empire in Southeast Asia many hundreds of years ago (see page 132). The remainder is made up mostly of Vietnamese, Chinese, and members of isolated hill tribes.

The vast majority of Cambodians have lived in villages of one kind or another. Village life followed the same rhythm of farming season and leisure season all over Southeast Asia.

A typical Cambodian village centered around a market place, where many residents gathered daily to trade, gossip, eat, laugh, and sing. A second important focus of village life was the *wat*, the Buddhist temple. Most Cambodians were devout Buddhists. And most male Cambodians spent at least a few months of their lives as Buddhist monks.

Because of its position at the center of the Indochina struggle, Cambodia has not escaped the pressures of a divided world. Its traditional customs and values remain strong, but new elements have been introduced: fear and distrust; pain, death, and hatred. Into this land of easygoing people, the modern world has forced its way with bewildering speed. Today few Cambodians can say, "Our bowl is always full."

Double-check

Review

1. The Vietnamese borrowed ideas and traits from which groups?

2. What is the traditional Vietnamese greeting?

3. Why do Vietnamese like to compare themselves to the bamboo plant?

4. At some point in his life, nearly every man or boy in Laos does what?

5. What did a typical Cambodian village center around?

Discussion

1. The culture of Indochina was greatly influenced by France, India, and China. What cultures do you think most influenced the U.S.? Give examples to support your answer. Do you think it is contradictory for a former colony to keep the "mother culture"? Why, or why not?

2. How are American and Vietnamese cultures different? How are they similar?

3. In a typical Laotian village, most of the people are related. How might this affect the lives of Laotian villagers?

Activities

1. Some students might research and report on the life and teachings of Confucius, the Chinese philosopher whose teachings had considerable influence on the Vietnamese code of conduct.

2. Two small groups of students might hold an informal debate in front of the class on the following topic: "The philosophy, Whatever will be, will be, is a good (or bad) approach to life in Southeast Asia."

3. A committee of students might research and report on the amount and causes of starvation deaths in Cambodia since 1975, and on the international relief efforts to help save the Cambodian people from extinction.

Skills

RICE PRODUCTION IN INDOCHINA*

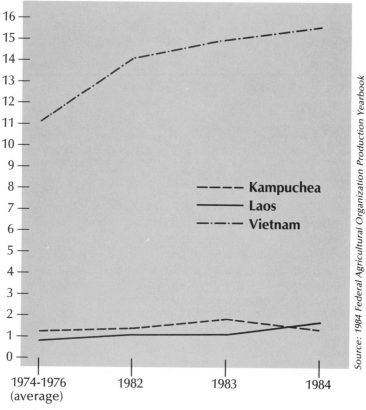

Source: 1984 Federal Agricultural Organization Production Yearbook

*in metric tons

Use the line graph above and information in Chapter 3 to answer the following questions.

1. What do the numbers on the left of the graph indicate?

2. Where did the information in this graph come from?

3. Which country appears to have consistently produced the most rice?

4. Which country's rice crop has declined?

5. What might be some reasons for a sharp drop in rice production?

Chapter 4

Malaysia and Singapore: Mixing Bowls of Southeast Asia

"WHOEVER KNOWS MALAYSIA has his hand on the pulse of Asia," runs a modern proverb which Malaysian leaders are fond of quoting. And the proverb appears to have a basis in truth.

Within its borders, Malaysia takes in a bewildering tangle of peoples and cultures. Malay fishermen, wealthy Indian and Pakistani rubber growers, tribesmen who only recently were headhunters, prosperous Chinese and British businessmen — all these and more are a part of the Malaysian scene.

The major reason for this variety is Malaysia's location. Malaysia stretches in a great broken arc from the tip of Thailand to the Philippine Islands (*see* map, page 53). It dominates the Straits of Malacca* and the South China Sea — the shortest sea route between the Indian and Pacific oceans. For hundreds of years, people traveling this great water highway have settled on these shores. Each new settlement added new blood. The result is the remarkably diverse population that makes up Malaysia today.

Three different states — Malaya, Sarawak,* and Sabah* — make up Malaysia. (Four lands made up the original Malaysia when it was formed in 1963, but Singapore left the Federation in 1965.) Time has been too short to merge all these diverse peoples, cultures, economies, and life-styles.

The heart of the Federation of Malaysia is Malaya, a fertile and mineral-rich peninsula about the size of Florida. Although 80 percent of its land is dense jungle, large rubber plantations and rich tin deposits have made Malaysia one of the wealthiest areas of Asia. More than one third of the world's natural rubber and one third of its tin come from Malaya.

Like Malaysia, Malaya is a mixing bowl of diverse peoples. Malay Moslems, who are fishermen and farmers, are the largest single group there. Next come the Chinese, many of whom operate shops and other businesses in the towns and cities. The descendants of Pakistanis and Indians who crossed the Indian Ocean many years ago to work on the rubber plantations now make up the third largest group.

Four hundred miles away from Malaysia are the two "poor cousins" of the Malaysian Federation—Sarawak and Sabah. Both are still made up mainly of vast stretches of unexplored jungles, mountains, and muddy rivers. With tiny Brunei—which became independent from British control at the end of 1983—the two states stretch over one quarter of the island of Borneo. The rest of Borneo is part of Indonesia.

The coastal areas of Sarawak and Sabah are partially developed. Isolated rubber and coconut plantations have been hacked out of the jungle. Towns have grown up around many of the larger plantations.

But the interior is a great unknown. There are vir-

52

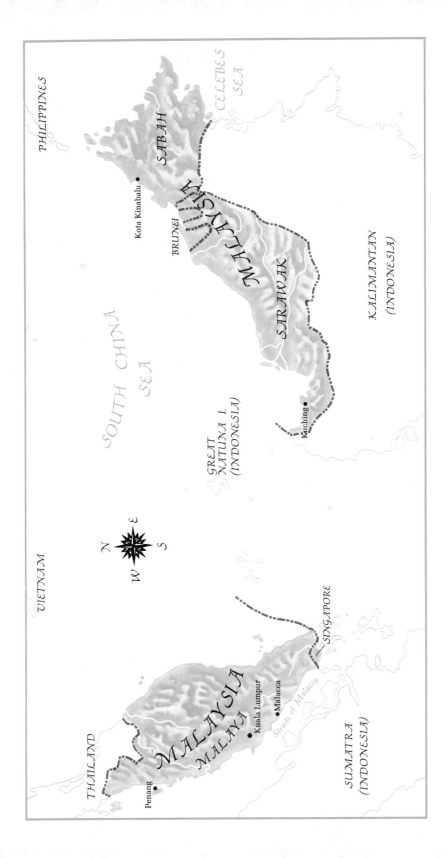

◄§ Many of the people of Singapore feel a deep attachment to China as their homeland.

tually no roads or bridges and only a few footpaths through the jungles. Rivers are the only dependable means of transportation.

The task of welding such a varied population spread over such a wide area is enormous. Other newly emerging countries have been split apart because their peoples could not get along together. Indeed, Malaysia's greatest problem is its cultural divisions. The wall of hostility and distrust is especially high between the country's Malays and Chinese.

The Malays and the Chinese are divided by religion, culture, and living standards. Each community fears the other will try to dominate it. Many of the Malays feel that they are shut out of business and the professions by the economic dominance of the Chinese. Many Chinese, especially the young, resent the political dominance of the Malays.

Malaysians, then, are a people of almost unequaled variety. This could be a fatal weakness to the country. Or it could be a source of strength.

☆ ☆ ☆ ☆ ☆ ☆ ☆ ☆ ☆

At the tip of the Malay Peninsula is the populous island nation of Singapore (see map, page 53). Its fine harbor and strategic position have made it one of the busiest ports in Asia. For more than a century, tin and rubber from Malaya, lumber from Borneo, and

In the island nation of Singapore, even show business has a Chinese touch. Here a singer in a Chinese street opera dons the costume he will use in his performance.

rubber, petroleum, tin, spices, and tobacco from Indonesia have poured into Singapore to be refined, packaged, or crated — and then shipped to the major markets of the Western world. Singapore is also the "Wall Street" of Southeast Asia. Its banks finance industries throughout the region.

Singapore is basically a Chinese city. More than three out of every four of the two-and-a-half million Singaporians are of Chinese origin.

Not surprisingly, most of the people of Singapore owe their livelihood to the island nation's strategic location. Many are in some aspect of commerce — as bankers and business promoters, as buyers and sellers of cargoes, as shopkeepers and longshoremen.

Singapore doesn't have much manufacturing, although this is growing. And with a size of about 226 square miles (about one fifth the size of Rhode Island), the island doesn't have room for farming.

Difficulty and uncertainty marked the initial years of Singapore's separation from the Federation of Malaysia in 1965. The government faced the problems that rapid population increase and slow industrialization in the island nation brought — inadequate housing, low income level and a high rate of unemployment especially among its restless young people. They blamed the government when they could not find jobs. There was also the problem of building loyalty to the idea of Singapore as a nation. Many of the people of Chinese origin in Singapore felt a deep attachment to China as their homeland. A program of priorities was introduced and today Singapore is among the more politically and economically stable nations in the area.

Double-check

Review

1. What three states make up Malaysia?

2. What has made Malaysia one of the wealthiest areas of Asia?

3. What is Malaysia's greatest problem?

4. Why is Singapore known as the "Wall Street" of Southeast Asia?

5. About what proportion of Singaporians are of Chinese origin?

Discussion

1. Like Malaysia, the United States has a variety of peoples and cultures. What are some of the differences and similarities between Malaysia's and the U.S.'s culture mix? Sometimes the U.S. is called a "melting pot," and Malaysia is called a "mixing bowl." What is the difference between these two metaphors? Are they accurate? Why, or why not?

2. Many people in Singapore blamed the goverment when they could not find jobs. Under what circumstances do you think people are justified in blaming their government if they cannot find work? When are they not justified? Give reasons to support your answers.

3. Many of Singapore's people felt a deep attachment to China, their country of origin. To which country should immigrants feel most loyal—their old country or their new country? Why?

Activities

1. Some students might role-play a discussion of the problems between Chinese and native-born Malaysians.

2. The population density in Singapore is 10,752 people per square mile. Some students might research and report on some of the recent studies on the physical and psychological effects of such extreme crowding.

3. Some students might draw posters or write make-believe radio ads prepared by the governments of Singapore and Malaysia in their efforts to increase the national loyalty of their diverse peoples.

Skills

LIVING AREA IN SOUTHEAST ASIA*

Country	Area (sq. miles)	Population density (1984 estimates)
BURMA	261,789	139.2
BRUNEI	2,226	97.9
CAMBODIA**	69,898	90
INDONESIA	741,101	221
LAOS	91,428	47.2
MALAYSIA	127,316	119
PHILIPPINES	115,831	459
SINGAPORE	239	10,582
THAILAND	198,500	254
VIETNAM	127,207	455

Source: The 1986 World Almanac

*People per square mile   **Democratic Kampuchea

Use the table above and information in Chapter 4 to answer the following questions.

1. Where did the information in this table come from?

2. For what year are the population density figures valid?

3. Which is the largest country in Southeast Asia? Which is the smallest?

4. Which is the most crowded country in Southeast Asia? Which is the least crowded?

5. Which Southeast Asian country is roughly twice the size of Rhode Island?

Chapter 5

Indonesia and the Philippines: Emeralds on the Blue

WHEN IT COMES to sprawling countries, Indonesia must be the "sprawlingest" of them all. It is one of the biggest island nations in the world, and all of it comes in bits and pieces.

From the Indian Ocean to the South Pacific, the 13,677 Indonesian islands and islets string out over more than 3,000 miles. (This is about the distance from New York to Ireland—as a very determined sea gull flies.) A catalogue of the 13,677 Indonesian islands and islets, of which 6,000 are inhabited, would include:

Three large islands: Sumatra,* Java, and Sulawesi.* (The last is still identified on some maps by its old name, Celebes.*)

Parts of two islands: the Indonesian parts of Borneo (now called Kalimantan*) and West New Guinea* (renamed Irian Jaya*).

Some 13,677 other islands and islets of assorted sizes. If all these islands could somehow be shoved together, the resulting lump of land would add up to an area about one-fifth that of the U.S.

Some of this land amounts to little more than volcanic lava. But much of it consists of lush, green tropical islands with soil so rich that practically any sort of tropical plant will thrive. Scratch the surface of Indonesia's soil and there are other natural treasures: oil, tin, coal, iron ore, bauxite.

Just as the Indonesian landscape varies, so do the local ways and customs which survive there. Religion is a case in point. People of Java — which is where most Indonesians live — are mostly Moslems. But right next door, on the smaller island of Bali, most of the people are Hindus.

Some of Indonesia's most isolated people are to be found deep in the forests of Kalimantan. Here families live in long houses on stilts. Their diet consists largely of dry rice and the meat of deer, hunted with blowpipes and poison-tipped darts. Their livelihood comes from collecting the many forest products — such as timber — for shipment to the cities.

The roots of Indonesia's diversity lie largely in its rich historical heritage, which could be compared to a layer cake. For centuries upon centuries, people have migrated to these lovely, inviting islands. Each wave of migration has left its mark, piling one cultural layer upon another.

Very little is known of the original inhabitants of the Indonesian islands. Probably about 5,000 years ago, these people began to be overwhelmed by migrating Malays from the Asian mainland. It is these Malays who today make up the basic stock of the Indonesian people. Around the time of Christ, traders and travelers from India arrived. They brought with them their Hindu faith.

Hindu kingdoms were first established on the is-

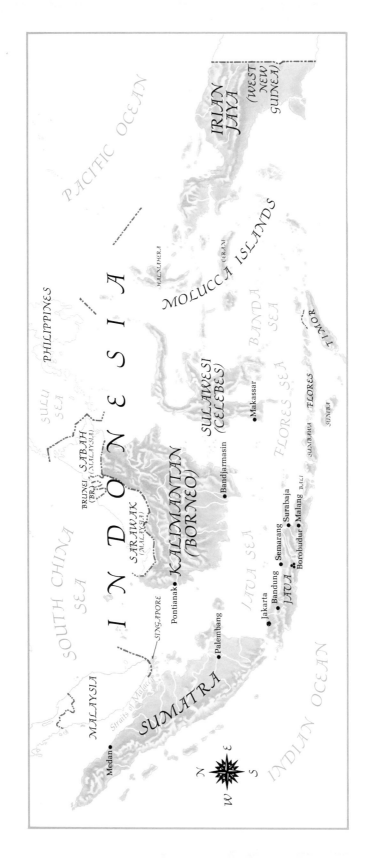

ᨠᨢ More than 60 percent of Indonesia's population is jammed onto Java.

land of Sumatra, and then spread to Java. Late in the 13th century, a Java-based kingdom called Maja-pahit* began to carve out a mighty empire.

Through all this, the intermingling of peoples went on. People came from south China and from the states of Southeast Asia. They came from as far away as Arabia and Persia. In many parts of Indonesia, Hinduism gave way to Buddhism. It, in turn, was re-placed by the Islamic faith of the Arab seafarers. Islam remains Indonesia's dominant religion today. But it is a very different faith from that which is fol-lowed in the Middle East. In many parts of Indonesia, the threads of the earlier Buddhist and Hindu faiths have been woven into the Islamic fabric.

By the 16th century, the great empire of Majapa-hit had splintered into dozens of small kingdoms. Weakened by divisions, the East Indies and its riches became easy pickings for the Europeans.

The period of colonial rule in Southeast Asia is not a part of this chapter (see page 137). It is enough to note that the Dutch began taking control of the East Indies in the late 16th century and held it, except for a few brief periods, until 1949. In that year, after a bloody colonial war and rising world pressure, the Dutch departed and Indonesia became independent.

Until independence, the question "What is an In-donesian?" hardly troubled the Indonesians them-selves. Indonesians were simply people who lived on a group of islands controlled by the Dutch. But with

Traffic creeps into Jakarta, Indonesia's capital and one of the world's most populous cities.

the departure of the Dutch, Indonesian leaders were faced with the problem of giving their people a sense of national identity.

This proved difficult. Not only is Indonesia spread out over a wide area, its population is unevenly distributed. More than 60 percent of Indonesians live on Java, making it one of the most densely populated spots on earth. Other Indonesian islands are practically deserted. New Guinea, for example, has only five people per square mile. The government has tried unsuccessfully to convince some of the Javanese to move to other islands.

Nation-building ran up against other problems. There are vast differences of culture, wealth, and education between people. These differences were compounded by the fact that Indonesians speak more than 250 languages and dialects. In many cases, the language of one group could not be understood by a neighboring group.

Since independence, Indonesia has tried to unite its people by adopting a national language, "Bahasa Indonesia." It is based mainly on the Maylay language. Today, most Indonesians can speak this language, even if they speak a local language at home.

Another challenge for Indonesia has been education. In 1945, only 10 percent of its people could read and write. Today, more than 90 percent of its children attend school. There they learn to read and write Bahasa Indonesia. Higher education is a bigger problem. At each step—junior high, high school, and college—there are fewer and fewer students.

Slowly but surely, Indonesia is building unity from its diversity. Although economic prosperity has been slow in coming, it seems to be on the rise.

☆ ☆ ☆ ☆ ☆ ☆ ☆ ☆ ☆

You can get a quick lesson in the cultural heritage of the Philippines by reading street signs in the country's

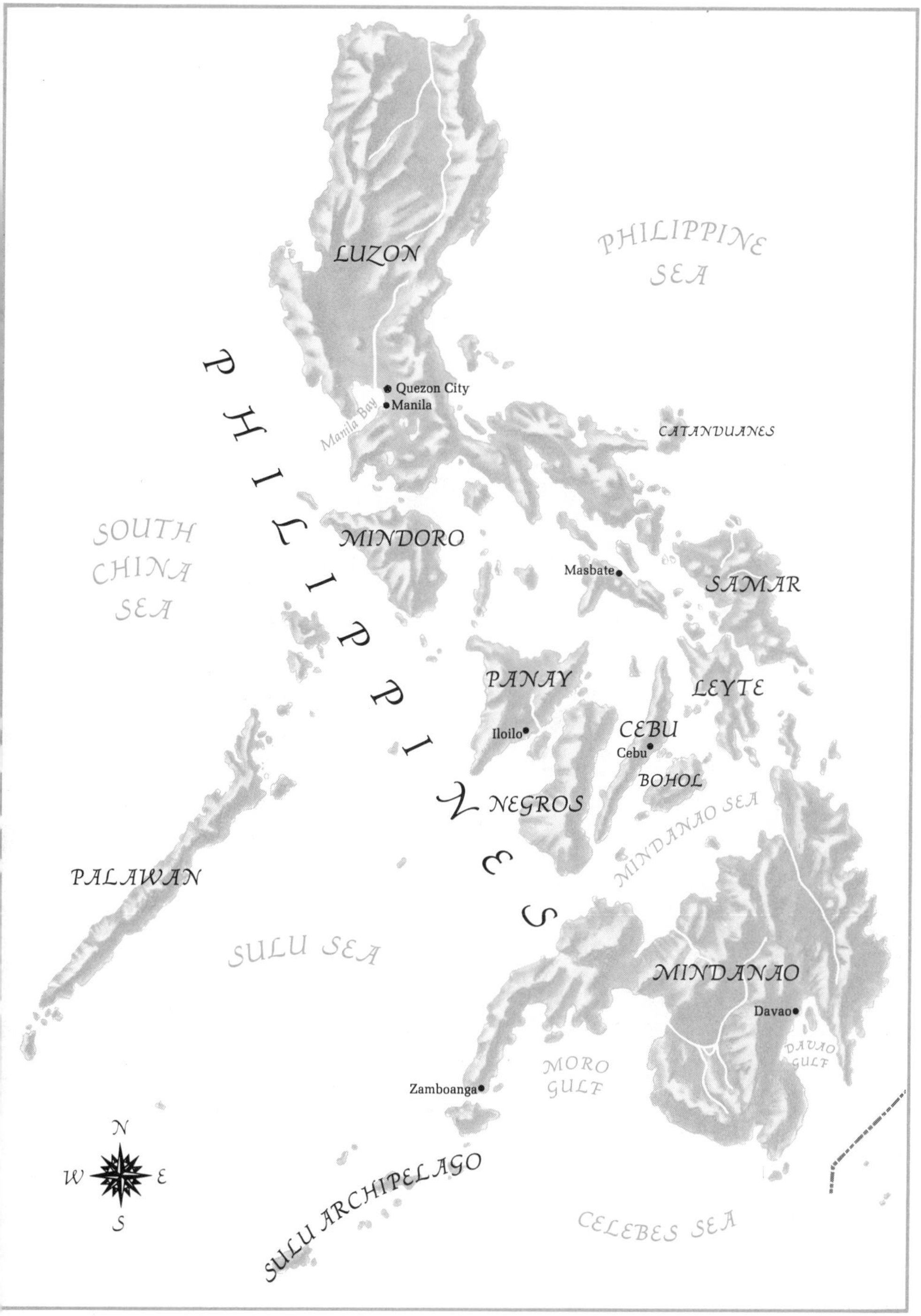

PHILIPPINES
LUZON
PHILIPPINE SEA
Quezon City
Manila
Manila Bay
CATANDUANES
SOUTH CHINA SEA
MINDORO
Masbate
SAMAR
PANAY
LEYTE
Iloilo
CEBU
Cebu
BOHOL
NEGROS
MINDANAO SEA
PALAWAN
SULU SEA
MINDANAO
Davao
DAVAO GULF
MORO GULF
Zamboanga
N
W
E
S
SULU ARCHIPELAGO
CELEBES SEA

largest city, Manila. You find a street named Bambang, from the national language called Pilipino* and Spanish names like San Luis and San Marcelino. There are Chicago Street and Taft Avenue, named for William Howard Taft, who was governor general of the Philippines before he became President of the United States.

The street signs are a reminder of the three strong influences of Phillipine culture. Pilipino is spoken by many people on the island of Luzon* where Manila is located. Spain took over the Phillipines in the 1500's and held it until 1898. During this period, Spanish became a widely used second language. A great many Filipinos became Roman Catholics and adopted Spanish names.

Then, as a result of victory in the Spanish-American War, the United States took control of the Phillipines. American businesspeople set up companies in the islands. American teachers taught in the schools, and American officials helped administer the Phillipine government. The Philippines won independence in 1946, but both Spanish and American influences remained strong.

The Phillipines is an island nation. Like a broken string of emerald beads, the more than 7,000 Phillipine islands lie scattered across the Western Pacific. Fewer than 500 of the islands are larger than one square mile in area, and only about 700, or one in 10, have anybody living on them. Most of the islands are so tiny they don't even have names.

Yet many of the islands are fertile and rich in natural resources. The land of the Phillipines is highly suitable

Many Filipino fishermen "farm" the seas in canoes called bancas. In what ways do you suppose this family, pictured aboard a houseboat, has turned its surroundings to its own advantage?

for farming. The rich soil and tropical climate also supports extensive timber growth. Iron ore, manganese, gold, copper, and other minerals are mined. Untapped wealth from the earth is one of the keys to the Phillipines' future.

Today, three out of every five Filipinos live in the villages (called barangay*, in recognition of the traditional political structure before the coming of the Spaniards), where most of them work in some form of agriculture. Let's look at a typical barangay.

The average barangay consists of about 200 families. Three-fourths of the men are farmers, who usually produce only enough to feed their own households. Most families live in thatched houses, set up on stilts so that they won't be flooded out during the rainy season. Most have no plumbing.

In most barangays, despite an occasional gasoline pump or generator, the primary source of "horsepower" is the *carabao*.* It is a water buffalo with a smooth skin and a liking for cooling off from the tropical heat by wadding nose-deep in streams and rivers. To those families that have them, carabaos usually are considered a prized possession, for they help with the plowing.

The other face of life in the Philippines is in the cities. If life in the barangay has not changed all that much over the centuries, life in the Philippine cities has, especially in the past two decades. Downtown Manila, for example, with its broad boulevards and gleaming hotels, has all the conveniences and inconveniences of any U.S. city.

But Manila, with its riches, is also the site of some of the world's worst slums. The very rich and the very poor sometimes live within sight of each other, with the latter far outnumbering the former. In the worst slums, many squatters live in shacks patched together from the old cardboard.

Despite the vicious poverty in Manila and other Philippine cities, people still come to the cities from the rural barangay. That is because the cities are seen more than ever before as places of opportunity. Some ambitious young people from the barangays go there to get work, any work at all.

Although the Philippines is divided by its many islands, there are several elements holding this young nation together. Among these is the relative cultural unity of the people. Most Filipinos are of Malay stock, with some Spanish blood mixed in.

There is also a sprinkling of Chinese, Indian, and Arabian blood in today's Filipino. There are an estimated one million Chinese, most of them engaged in commerce in the cities.

Another unifying factor is religion. Most Filipinos are Roman Catholics, and the Philippines is the only Southeast Asian country in which Christianity is the major religion.

But perhaps, the most important unifying factor in the Philippines is the feeling of nationhood. This young country, proud as it is of its Spanish heritage and long-time association with the United States, is ever prouder of its existence as an independent nation of Southeast Asia.

Double-check

Review

1. The roots of Indonesia's diversity lie largely in what?

2. With the departure of the Dutch, Indonesian leaders were faced with what problem?

3. The street signs of Manila are a reminder of what?

4. The U.S. took control of the Philippines as a result of what event?

5. What is a *barangay*?

Discussion

1. In your opinion, would Americans have as much difficulty answering the question, "What is an American?" as Indonesians have in answering the question, "What is an Indonesian?" Why, or why not? How would you answer the first question? How would you answer the second question?

2. The island of Java is crowded with 60 percent of Indonesia's population, while many other Indonesian islands are almost deserted. What problems might this cause for the nation? Do you think something should be done to redistribute the population? Why, or why not? Can you think of a program to redistribute people that would not restrict their freedom? If you lived on Java, how might you be convinced to move to a less-populous island?

3. Is life in a Philippine *barangay* different from or similar to life in your community? Explain. Would you prefer living in a place where life is fast-paced, or in a place where life changes slowly? Why?

Activities

1. A few students might role-play Indonesian political candidates debating the topic: "How to give Indonesia a sense of national identity."

2. Some students might research and report on the *barangay* as the typical Philippine political structure before the Spaniards came.

3. Some students might pretend to be young people from *barangays* who arrive in Manila and cannot find work. They should write letters about their experiences to their make-believe family back home. They might then read their letters aloud in class.

Skills

INDONESIA'S RELIGIONS

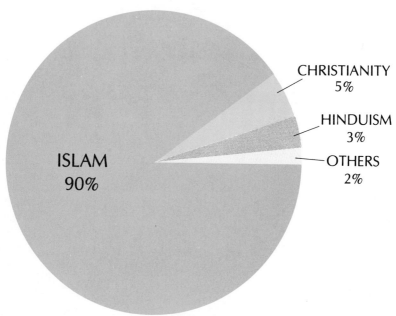

Source: *The Statesman's Yearbook, 1979–80*

Use the circle graph above and information in Chapter 5 to answer the following questions.

1. According to this graph, at least how many different religions are practiced in Indonesia?

  (a) three   (b) four   (c) two

2. A quick glance at this graph shows that the overwhelming majority of Indonesians practice which religion?

  (a) Hinduism   (b) Christianity   (c) Islam

3. What percentage of Indonesians follow the second most common religion in their country?

  (a) 90 percent   (b) five percent   (c) two percent

4. It is probably safe to assume that fewer than what percentage of Indonesians practice Buddhism?

  (a) one percent   (b) zero percent   (c) two percent

5. What percentage of Indonesians follow the major religion of the Philippines?

  (a) five percent   (b) three percent   (c) two percent

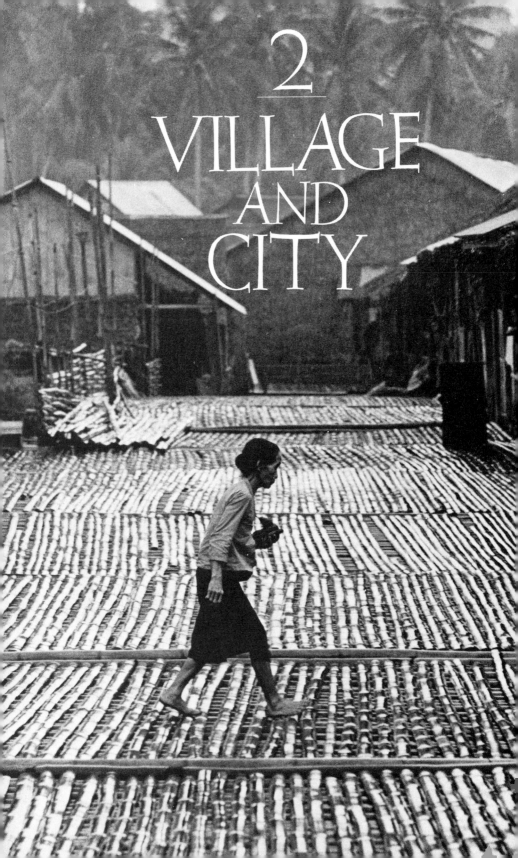

2
VILLAGE AND CITY

Chapter 6

Village Life

SOMETIMES ON MAY NIGHTS, Hla* lies awake and listens. If he waits long enough, what he expects often happens. Gently at first but with thickening force, the rain comes splattering down on the thatched roof above his head. Then Hla's sleeping village on the banks of the Irrawaddy River in central Burma becomes a world of splashing noise.

To Hla the first rains of May have a cheerful sound. As they beat downward, life seems to begin anew. Soon the rains will dress his village in a coat of brilliant green. And they will pave the way for the work which Hla, his father, and his younger brother have to do.

For months the ground around Hla's village has lain brown and unused. The hot sun has burned down day after day. The earth has formed a hard crust in which no crops will grow. Now the monsoon rains will loosen the soil and make planting possible.

To hasten the process, the farmers will churn up the earth of the rice fields. Slowly the soil will turn to mud. When the mud is soft enough, the farmers will sink the roots of their rice shoots into it. Then they will wait and watch the rice shoots grow.

This method has been passed from generation to generation for hundreds of years. Hla, who is now 14, has been learning it since he was old enough to walk. His father has patiently taught him how to grow rice shoots from seed, how to transplant the tender shoots to the fields, and how to harvest the crop when it has turned to a brilliant gold.

This has not been Hla's only education. When he was younger, he attended his village school and learned to read and write. But he considers his father's lessons in the muddy fields the most important ones of all. For they will help him to make his way in the village where he plans to spend his life.

In his 14 years Hla has grown familiar with his small village in nearly every detail. He has counted every tinkling bell in the Buddhist temple where his family worships. He has learned to watch out for every rut in the unpaved village roads. He loves his village and cannot imagine living anywhere else.

Hla's house is a cottage at the center of the village. It sits on a raised platform with a floor of split bamboo. The house has little furniture, since the Burmans sit on mats on the floor. The house also has no electricity or plumbing. After dark, the family sees by the light of a small fire which glows throughout the night.

Hla has been away from home only once. Two years ago, when he was 12, he went off for three months to a nearby Buddhist monastery to become a novice (beginner) in his faith (see page 162). At first Hla thought the trip was exciting. But after a few

When the monsoon rains come, work goes on from dawn to dusk. In unison with one another, Southeast Asian women transfer young rice plants into fields flooded by the monsoons.

weeks he came down with a severe case of homesickness. He was glad when his stay in the monastery was over and he could return to his family.

The family has six members — Hla, his mother and father, his two older sisters, and his younger brother. Like most Burmans, Hla's parents don't consider their more distant relatives such as aunts and uncles to be a part of the basic family unit. Instead, they value the family as a close-knit group, tied together by feelings of mutual respect.

When Hla was younger, he showed his respect in the usual Burman way. Before bedtime prayers, he *shikkoed** — that is, he folded his hands and bowed so low that his forehead touched the floor. The first bow went to his father, the second to his mother. His parents responded: "May your holiness be great and your life long, may you be united with your parents even until the attainment of old age."

Now that Hla is older he no longer makes this formal gesture. But he still tries to be an obedient son. His father, in turn, is proud to be raising two boys of his own. He has corrected his sons on occasion, but he has never severely punished them.

Nor has he tried to boss his wife. The dominant role of men in other parts of East Asia does not necessarily apply in Burma — and not at all in Hla's family. His mother, like most Burman women, is highly independent. She is ready to listen to suggestions but not to take orders from her husband. In the same way, she is careful never to threaten her husband's *hpon** — his maleness — by forcing her wishes onto him.

Hla's mother, Mya,* did not take her husband's name when she married. Like all Burmans, she uses her given name without any family name at all. The Burmans do not pass family names down from one generation to the next. So the names of Hla's brothers and sisters give no clue that they are even related to one another.

Instead, each of them has a prefix which goes before his or her given name. Hla's prefix at the moment is "Maung," meaning "young brother." In a few years Maung Hla will probably be called U Hla — if he makes his mark as a farmer. "U" (meaning "uncle") is a term of address used to signify respect.

The happiest moments for Hla's family come in late autumn when the skies of Burma sparkle and the air is dry once more. The autumn sun has turned the rice fields to gold, and now harvest time is here.

Early every morning the villagers go out to the fields — the men to do the reaping, the women to tie the rice stalks in bundles. If the harvest is a good one, the villagers are in a merry mood. They chatter gaily to one another as they go about their work.

The first of the rice crop is offered to the Buddhist monks in nearby villages. The rest is kept for the family or sent to market to be sold. Once the entire harvest is in, Hla and his family can pause in their labors for several months. They will not begin another planting season until the monsoon rains come splattering down again the following May.

☆ ☆ ☆ ☆ ☆ ☆ ☆ ☆ ☆

Siti* has never been to Burma. She would probably be surprised at Hla's dependence on the monsoon rains. Her village on the Indonesian island of Bali does not rely on the monsoon season for growing. Along the sloping terraces near her home, rice grows at any time of year.

At 15, Siti has learned a lot about rice farming. She and her mother often work out in the terraced rice fields while her father tends to other matters. He is a village artisan, and he concentrates on carving figures out of stone.

His work is not unusual. Even in the smallest Balinese communities, painting, sculpting, and wood carving have a very wide appeal. Siti's father carves animals out of stone. He digs his stone from a nearby river bed and then works it with a special knife.

He sells some of his sculpture to local customers. But nowadays most of his customers are travelers to Bali from the United States and Western Europe. These people come on vacation to bask in the island's tropical sun. Some of them who visit Siti's village buy some of her father's sculptures.

Siti tries to be hospitable to the Westerners, but she really finds them puzzling. In the first place, she is amused by the clothes the Western men wear. Ba-

linese men wear loose skirts called *sarongs*,* splashed
with the deepest reds, blues, and greens. They make
even the most colorfully dressed Westerners look a
little pale.

Even more puzzling is the behavior of these customers. Sometimes, Siti has noticed, they get angry
when her father refuses to lower the price of his artwork. In Balinese tradition, the ability to stay cool
and collected is a mark of dignity. So such flashes of
temper strike Siti as being very impolite.

Several times Siti has tried in her broken English to give Westerners a tour of her family compound. This is a cluster of thatched-roof dwellings shared by several generations of her family. Surrounding the compound is a wall of mud and thatch which stands two feet thick and five feet high. Siti's family believes that the wall keeps away evil spirits, who cannot climb that high. But Westerners usually think of it as a protection against burglars.

Westerners seem interested in the small shrines which decorate the compound's courtyard. These shrines honor a number of different spirits. One serves the spirits of the ancestors. Another serves the spirit of the land the compound stands on. Two others serve the spirits of Bali's two sacred volcanoes, Agung* and Batur,* which rise in barren splendor at the eastern edge of the island.

Several tourists have asked Siti why her family worships so many spirits. The answer is rooted in the island's past. For centuries, most Balinese have been Hindus. But they have also interwoven some animism and some ancestor worship into the many strands of their belief (see Chapter 14).

Bali's major spirits are said to live amid the peaks of its two loftiest volcanoes. Its demons are thought to make their home in the surrounding sea.

Partly for that reason, the Balinese take little delight in the roaring ocean surf. Unlike most island peoples, they regard the sea with dread. Siti has watched Western tourists sunbathing on the white sands of Bali's southern coast, but she has never joined them. She is frightened by the huge breakers which pound the barrier reef a few yards from shore.

What has startled Siti the most about these sun-loving Westerners is their attitude toward the most sacred Balinese ceremonies. Her puzzlement stems

from an incident which took place a few months ago. At the time, Siti had just entered her adulthood. She had done so through a ceremony to protect her against sadripu,* the evil in human nature.

The coming-of-age ritual involves the filing of the front teeth by a local Hindu priest. The purpose of this ritual is religious. Balinese who have filed teeth believe they will be accepted by the gods. Those who do not, fear they will be mistaken for fanged demons.

At the end of the ceremony, Siti was relieved. She felt that her teeth were more attractive, and she had suffered no pain at all. She also felt more religious and truly more adult. As she left the ceremony, she flashed her widest smile.

It was just then, in the courtyard, that the incident took place. She heard one Western tourist turn to the other and say, "Well, that's one way to clean your teeth." The wisecrack wasn't meant to insult Siti. Still, it offended her.

Siti has tried to dismiss the incident with an old Indonesian saying: "Other fields, other locusts; other pools, other fish." Siti thinks of this saying as one of tolerance toward others, and she has tried to remember it. She thinks some of her island's many tourists should learn the phrase as well.

Balinese girls head for temple, balancing rice cakes and flowers, gifts they will offer to the gods.

Double-check

Review

1. How does Hla's family see after dark?

2. What happens to the first of the rice crop in Burma?

3. What do most Balinese men wear?

4. What is a mark of dignity in Bali?

5. Bali's demons are thought to make their home where?

Discussion

1. Burmese do not have "family" or "last" names. How might this affect social life in Burma? What kinds of things would become more or less important?

2. Many Balinese believe in spirits or demons. What kinds of superstitions do people in our society believe in? Why do you think people believe in superstitions? What might be beneficial about such beliefs? What might be harmful about such beliefs?

3. In Burma, the work cycle follows the cycle of the seasons. Is this true for most work in your community? How is life different for families whose work cycles are not tied to nature and the seasons? Would you prefer work that depended on the seasons, or work that did not depend on the seasons? Why?

Activities

1. Some students might research and report to the rest of the class on the order and significance of ways in which names are put together in various cultures. Students in the class might then try arranging their own names in the different customs described.

2. A committee of students might look through U.S. history books and other books with illustrations of past centuries to find how fashion in the U.S. has changed through the centuries. They might draw men's and women's fashions from each century and use the drawings in a bulletin board display.

3. Several students might pretend to be Siti writing a response to the Western tourist who offended her. In the letter, the students could explain why the coming-of-age ritual is important to Siti and how the remark makes her feel.

Skills

Readers' Guide to Periodical Literature

March 1977 – February 1978

Page 180

BUDDHA and Buddhism
Buddhism: the middle way. il Sr Schol 109:24-6 + F 24 '77
Tovil: exorcism by white magic; ceremony of Sri Lanka's Buddhists. M. M. Ames. il Natur Hist 87:42-9 bibl (p 108) Ja '78
See also
Monasteries, Buddhist

Study and teaching
Precious master of the mountains; Naropa Institute. il por Time 109:86 F 14 '77

BUDDHISM and Christianity. See Christianity and other religions

BUDDHIST literature
Art of dying; Tibetan book of the dead. D. Goleman. Psychol Today 10:58-9 Ap '77

BUDDHIST monasteries. See Monasteries, Buddhist

Abbreviations

Ap — April

bibl — bibliography

F — February

il — illustrated

Ja — January

Natur Hist — *Natural History*

por — Portrait

Psychol Today — *Psychology Today*

Sr Schol — *Senior Scholastic*

+ — continued on later pages

Use the above listings from Readers' Guide to Periodical Literature *and information in Chapter 6 to answer the following questions.*

1. In which of the following publications will you find the articles listed in *Readers' Guide?*
(a) newspapers (b) magazines (c) books

2. How many articles are listed above?
(a) four (b) five (c) nine

3. How long a period of time is covered by this edition of *Readers' Guide?*
(a) two years (b) two months (c) one year

4. An article in which publication contains a bibliography?
(a) *Senior Scholastic* (b) *Natural History* (c) *Time*

5. Under which letter of the alphabet would you look in *Readers' Guide* for an article about where Hla spent three months when he was 12?
(a) M (b) C (c) S

Chapter 7

City Life

ALONG THE MUDDY CANALS of Bangkok, Thailand, people start their days at dawn. As the hot sun creeps up into the sky, the slumbering city comes to life. Blunt-nosed sampans glide gracefully downstream, delivering fruits and vegetables to market. Water taxis shuttle about the city, taking tourists to see the sights.

At dawn the narrow waterways have a peaceful look. Yet these hours are worrisome for 13-year-old Anek Thamthiangsat.* At that time of day Bangkok's boatmen are sleepiest, and they sometimes lose control of their sampans. In the past few weeks two of them have scraped the sides of Anek's father's boat.

The boat is nothing fancy. It is a ramshackle old vessel made of scraps of teakwood with a rusted tin roof for shelter at the rear. It is about twice as long as, and not much wider than, an ordinary rowboat. Still,

Anek has good reason to worry, for this simple little houseboat is his home.

He and his family do not live there for adventure. It is the best accommodation they can obtain for the little money they have. Anek's father loads cargoes by hand aboard ships in the harbor. His is a sweaty, backbreaking job, and it brings him barely enough income to support his family. As he sometimes jokes, he is only just managing to keep his family afloat.

Mr. Thamthiangsat keeps his houseboat tied to a post at the side of one of Bangkok's busier canals. These canals, called *klongs*, flow out of the Chao Phraya River at the center of the city. From the Chao Phraya some klongs meander their way to outlying rice fields where they irrigate the soil. Once in a while, Anek and his family paddle up a klong to the countryside on a pleasure trip.

But such trips are rare these days. Anek's father has been too busy working overtime to support his family's needs. Once a day Anek's mother takes the boat to a floating market where she buys food from surrounding sampans. Otherwise, the family's boat usually stays tied up in its klong.

Aboard the boat, Anek, his younger sister, and his parents live in very close quarters. They cook their meals over charcoal fires and eat while sitting or crouching on deck. They sleep on deck too, stowing their bedding under the tin roof during the day. They wash laundry in the klong and spread it on top of the roof to dry. Their routine allows them little privacy, but it is the only life they know.

Anek has lived this way as long as he can remember. His father bought the houseboat at the time Anek was born. In those days Mr. Thamthiangsat thought the boat would be only a temporary home — to be used until he found more spacious quar-

ᴥᵹ **Aboard the boat, Anek
and his family live in
very close quarters.**

*Sampans loaded with fruits and vegetables are
typical of Bangkok's floating markets. Here
Thai "shopkeepers" wait patiently on the
klong for their daily customers to arrive.*

ters. Now he knows there's little hope of moving and
has resigned himself to living out his life along the
klong.

Anek has some idea of what it must be like to live
in fancier surroundings. He has seen several of the
Bangkok palaces whose needle-thin spires jab the

city skyline. Anek particularly likes to visit the grounds of the Grand Palace, a fairyland of steep-roofed and spired buildings, rimmed by thick walls.

On his trips to the Grand Palace, Anek has been especially fascinated by the buildings' outer walls. They are made of precious materials such as gold leaf, porcelain fragments, and mother-of-pearl. As a Buddhist, Anek should not be too impressed by such signs of wealth and power. But try as he may, he cannot help but wish he had money of his own.

Anek is ambitious. He knows that there is much more to life than working as a cargo-handler and living aboard a houseboat. He believes that the key to his future is an education — and he is getting one at a school in downtown Bangkok. After he turns 15, he will no longer be required by law to continue school, but he hopes to do so anyway. He wants to go to business school to study English and bookkeeping. After that, he will enter a Buddhist monastery for three months and then begin his business career.

His dream is to work in the office of a trading company. He wants to dress in a suit, with pens and pencils in his pocket and a watch on his wrist. More than that, he wants to give orders, make deals, talk on the telephone, and dictate to a secretary.

His father hasn't tried to discourage him. Yet Mr. Thamthiangsat knows how hard his son will have to work to reach this station in life. Though things are changing in Bangkok, it is still hard for young Thais to reach a higher status than that of their parents. There are tremendous pressures which keep most people "in their place."

Thus, Anek has a long uphill climb ahead of him. If he were rich or noble, the climb would be easier. As it is, the going will be rough. But Anek also knows that the journey won't begin for a few more years. Right now he still has time to enjoy the everyday blessings which life bestows.

And blessings there are. After all, Anek lives in a mild climate where life is leisurely. Lately he has even found a way of forgetting about traffic collisions in the klong. Every morning, when the sun burns hot across his houseboat, he plunges over the side. He kicks and splashes through the water for several minutes, turning over and over before rising, with a broad grin, onto the houseboat's bow.

☆ ☆ ☆ ☆ ☆ ☆ ☆ ☆ ☆

Beth Villahermosa* also likes to swim. But she does most of her bathing in the pastel blue waters of her private swimming pool. The pool sits snugly in the courtyard of her family's Spanish-style home near Manila in the Philippines. So Beth, 14, can get her exercise without ever leaving the house.

That is just the way Beth's father wants it. He has taken every step he can to insure Beth's safety. As a lawyer in the Philippine city of Manila, he is well aware of the high crime rate in the city. As the head of an old and wealthy family, he worries that some harm may come to his wife and two daughters.

Partly for this reason, the Villahermosa family lives in the "supersafe" community of Forbes Park. This suburb, a little east of downtown Manila, has been nicknamed "Millionaires' Row." Around the rim of the community stretches a tall barbed-wire fence. Gates are watched by private guards who carry guns.

Behind the gates rise the rambling houses of Manila's "big rich." Beth's is a large stone house with grilled windows and floors of bright red tile. The house has three stories with most of the ground floor used for servants' quarters and storage space. Behind the house are a stone terrace and a sweeping lawn.

✎ Beth knows Sofia's wedding will cost her father more money than many Filipinos earn in an entire year.

This lawn has been a busy place in the past few months. Almost a year ago, a neighbor, Emilio, began using it to court Beth's sister, Sofia. At first he would come alone to stand beneath Sofia's window, strum a guitar, and sing. As time went on, he brought several other men with him to join in the songs.

Sofia's mother and father were delighted by this Spanish custom, known as the *harana** (or serenade). They enjoyed Emilio's music, though Mr. Villahermosa joked that Emilio had no better singing voice than his own. At last, one evening, Sofia's mother and father invited the serenaders into the house for refreshments. Sofia started dating Emilio, and in time he coaxed her into agreeing to marriage. After that, his parents formally asked for her hand.

Since then, Sofia has been busily making wedding plans. The ceremony will take place in the Roman Catholic church a few blocks from Sofia's home in about two months. Sofia has chosen a date when the moon is in its last quarter. This is the time when weddings are said to bring the most happiness.

After the wedding, the bride and groom and 400 guests will hold a motorcade through the streets of the community to Sofia's home where they will have a giant feast in the backyard. The feast will feature a typical Filipino dish, *picadillo*,* made of tomatoes, potatoes and ground pork.

The climax of the reception will come after the feast. An orchestra of violins, guitars, and marimbas will strike up a tune on the terrace floor. Then Sofia

Tightly packed wooden shanties are home for these young residents of a Manila barrio. Behind the shanties rise newer and more solid-looking homes. How does this neighborhood contrast with the text description of "Millionaires' Row"?

and Emilio will perform a dance called the *pandanggo.** As they spin about the lawn, guests will pin gifts of money on the newlyweds' clothes.

All this excites Beth. Yet she has some nagging doubts about the party's size. She knows that the wedding will cost her father more money than many Filipinos earn in an entire year. She thinks Sofia's wedding plans are much too lavish when so many Filipinos are so poor.

Beth's concern for the poor has been mounting ever since she took an auto trip with her family a few months ago. On the way home from the trip, Beth's father made a wrong turn on the road. He ended up winding through the alleyways of Tondo,* a northern district of Manila. Beth had never before set eyes on the area, and she was horrified at what she saw.

Poverty had drawn a noose around the neighborhood. Squalid shacks of scrap lumber huddled together along the alleyways. Garbage lay uncollected in the dusty streets. Old men slept in doorways, their toothless mouths open wide. Small children went without a shred of clothing.

Back in Forbes Park, Beth could not put the nightmare of Tondo out of her mind. She began looking through the daily newspapers to find out more about Manila's slums. She learned that one out of every three people in Manila is a squatter such as those who live in Tondo. They own neither their homes nor the land the homes are built on.

Beth has tried discussing the problems of Manila's squatters with some of her teenage friends in Forbes Park. But she has been surprised at how few of these friends know anything at all about such problems.

As a result, Beth now believes that she and her friends have led a very sheltered life. She thinks they all should have much more concern for the poor.

So far she has kept her thoughts about Sofia's wedding to herself. She knows she must not criticize Sofia or her father in front of the other members of the family or her friends. But Beth has told herself that she would like a smaller wedding when she is married. And somehow she doesn't think she'll ever change her mind.

Double-check

Review

1. What size is Anek's family's boat?

2. Why do Anek and his family live in a houseboat?

3. What has Forbes Park been nicknamed?

4. What is a *harana?*

5. What is the percentage of squatters in Manila?

Discussion

1. What effect does "keeping people in their place" have on people? On a country as a whole?

2. Because crime is increasing in the city of Manila, many people who can afford it are moving to the "safe" suburbs. What new problems does such an exodus create for the city? What problems does it create for cities in the U.S.?

3. Would you, like Beth, feel inclined to criticize the cost of Sofia's wedding? Why, or why not? If so, how would you handle your feelings? Do you think Beth is right not to criticize Sofia or her father in front of the other members of the family or in front of her friends? What could Beth do *now* about the problems of poverty? What might she be able to do in the future? Give reasons to support your answers.

Activities

1. Some students might pretend to be Anek, writing in his diary about his future plans, hopes, and dreams. What might he hope for? What might be some difficulties he expects to face?

2. One half of the class might role-play young teenagers from a Manila *barrio*. The other half could be teenagers from Forbes Park. In a discussion between the groups, what might be said?

3. A person in your community who works to combat poverty and to help poor people might be invited to speak to the class about her or his work. Students might prepare a list of questions to ask the speaker before she or he visits the class.

Skills

USING AN INDEX

floating markets, 34, 85, 86*
Forbes Park, 88, 91
Four Truths, 160
France, influence in
  Indochina, 35, 40, 42,
  138,* 144, 153, 175

gamelan, 186
Geneva Agreements, 153,
  198, 199, 210
Goa, 139
government, 36, 145,
  149–155, 197, 199–202,
  217–218, 219, 229
Grand Palace, 87
guerrilla warfare, 149, 150,
  152, 153
Gulf of Siam, 34
Gulf of Tonkin resolution,
  199

Hanoi (North Vietnam), 42,
  145, 210, 212, 213
harana (defined), 89

*Photograph.

Use the above excerpt from the Index of this book and information in Chapter 7 to answer the following questions.

1. In what order are topics listed in an index?
  (a) alphabetically   (b) in order of importance   (c) by page numbers

2. What do the numbers after each topic stand for?
  (a) ages   (b) chapter references   (c) page references

3. On how many pages in this text is Forbes Park discussed?
  (a) four   (b) two   (c) 76

4. On which page would you find a photo of a market in Bangkok?
  (a) 86   (b) 32   (c) 123

5. On which page would you find the definition of a Spanish serenade?
  (a) 77   (b) 89   (c) 175

Chapter 8

Outsiders on the Inside

ONCE EVERY THREE OR FOUR MONTHS, Wu Hor Kar* gets to do one of the things she likes most. She and her family visit an amusement park near their home in Singapore. Late in the afternoon, Hor Kar buys an egg roll and climbs aboard the Ferris wheel. For the next 15 minutes she rides around and around by herself.

Though the Ferris wheel isn't particularly fast, it provides a spectacular view. At dusk the city of Singapore twinkles below like a magic carpet made of lights. From the top of the wheel, Hor Kar can see past the neon signs of the amusement park, past the glittering lights of Singapore's skyscrapers, out to the busy harbor and its great ships from every part of the world. Alone up there on the spinning wheel, Hor Kar gazes into space and dreams her private dreams.

Such moments are rare for Hor Kar. She doesn't have much time for daydreaming — or even for being alone. Raised in a family with three younger sisters and two younger brothers, she has always been surrounded by people. And her family has a special meaning for her, since the Wus are Chinese.

Like most people in Singapore, Hor Kar's mother and father call themselves *hua-chiao,** meaning "sojourning Chinese." A sojourner is a visitor who comes to a place for a while but doesn't mean to stay forever. Although the Wus have never been to China, they still think of it as home in some ways. They are tremendously proud of their cultural heritage from China. They keep this pride even though both sides of the family have lived in Southeast Asia for generations.

Hor Kar is 14 and has lived all of her life in Singapore. Her home is a neat white bungalow in a central section of the city. All around the Wus live other families of hua-chiao. The nearby markets are also run by Chinese.

Hor Kar's father is a sales agent for a large Chinese trading firm. He specializes in selling rubber from Malaysia and rice from Thailand. Mr. Wu spends part of each day talking long-distance on the telephone with rice traders in Bangkok. He can deal with these agents in his own language, for they are also of Chinese descent.

The hua-chiao are, in fact, scattered across Southeast Asia. They can be found in every country of the area and in many different walks of life. However, they face strong anti-Chinese feelings in many of these countries. And in the late 1970's, the governments of Vietnam and Cambodia expelled most hua-chiao.

In Singapore, many of the hua-chiao do work similar to Mr. Wu's. The city is the center of trade for Southeast Asia, and the Chinese make up more than 70 percent of the total population. Chinese businessmen have a reputation for being industrious — and Mr. Wu still more so. He plans some day to become a *towkay** — the Chinese word for one who manages his own business.

He also has high hopes for all his children. Year after year he has put up the money to send all six of them to private Chinese schools. Again and again he has urged them to apply themselves to their schoolwork. His urgings not only reflect his own ambition. They also reflect the emphasis placed on education within most Chinese families.

When it comes to schoolwork, Hor Kar gives her greatest attention to the languages she is taking. Singapore has four official languages — Malay, English, Chinese, and an Indian language called Tamil.* At the moment Hor Kar is learning all except Tamil. Chinese comes easiest to her since her family speaks it at home.

The Wus' belief in Chinese traditions goes farther than the matter of language. It also extends to the pattern of family relationships — with the eldest male as the undisputed head.

No member of Mr. Wu's household would dream of questioning his authority (though his wife sometimes tries to bend his wishes a little). The only family member who ever questions Hor Kar's father is her grandfather. When her grandfather comes to visit, *his* word is law.

As the eldest daughter, Hor Kar has some traditional family duties of her own. She is expected to help clean house and wash the dishes. She also "baby-sits" with her younger brothers and sisters when her mother goes to the market. If all goes as planned, she will soon start cooking some family din-

Chinese students at a Malaysian university give all their attention to answering an exam.

Mr. Wu has high hopes for his children. Year after year he has sent all six to private Chinese schools.

ners. Her mother has been teaching her the special skills of Chinese cooking.

At the moment Hor Kar's only future plans are to marry and raise a family of her own. She has not yet thought much about the kind of man she wants to marry — except to hope that he will be Chinese. Though her mother and father have not yet discussed the matter with her, she knows that they expect her to marry a Chinese man.

Her brothers have bigger plans. After finishing private school, they hope to go on to Nanyang* University in the western part of Singapore Island. Like the private school they are now attending, this university was started by the city's Chinese residents. Its name is the Chinese word for "Southern Ocean," the term the hua-chiao have given to Southeast Asia.

The ocean is an important symbol to many Chinese in Southeast Asia. For it plays a key role in the history of one of the largest groups of migrating people the modern world has seen. Ancestors of the hua-chiao arrived in the region after a long voyage across the sea. Only by recrossing the ocean can those who want to return to China ever make the trip.

Perhaps that is another reason why Hor Kar looks forward to her rides on the Ferris wheel. Up there at the top of the wheel, she can look out to the far horizon and study the contours of the sea. She feels certain she will live the rest of her life in Singapore. Yet she can dream of one day visiting China, where her cultural roots still lie.

☆ ☆ ☆ ☆ ☆ ☆ ☆ ☆ ☆

In many ways, David Chandy, who lives in Kuala Lumpur,* Malaysia — more than 200 miles north of

Rubber ranks as a valuable natural resource of Southeast Asia. Malaysian women of Indian descent are shown processing latex sheets.

98

Singapore — has much in common with Hor Kar. Both are 14, both speak more than one language, and both come from families with cultural ties to countries outside Southeast Asia. Hor Kar's ties are to China; David's are to India.

In fact, David was born in India — in the southern state of Madras, to be precise. He did not move to Kuala Lumpur until he was six years old. At that time David's father set up shop as a cloth merchant on one end of Jalan Petaling* (Petaling Street) in the Chinese quarter of the city. David soon became accustomed to his adopted city — "K.L.," as it is nicknamed — and now he calls it home.

In business, David's father handles many different kinds of fabrics. For example, he imports tie-dyed cloth from Madras and sells it to Indian women. They use the cloth for making saris* — floor-length garments which are wrapped around the waist and draped over one shoulder. Mr. Chandy also imports Indonesian fabrics known as batiks* and sells them to Malay customers. Malays use batiks for sarongs — loose skirts worn by both men and women.

The Chandy home sprawls across an acre of land on the outskirts of the city. It is a rambling one-story structure with a roof of bright red tile. Like much of "K.L.," the house is built on land reclaimed from the surrounding jungle. There are still traces of the jungle in the clumps of palm trees which stand serenely in the backyard.

Nearby is a rubber plantation where David often works in his spare time. His job is to load latex — the fluid from rubber trees — into pails and carry them to collection stations. The job is similar to the kind of work which Indians have done for generations. In fact, many of the million or so Indians of Malaysia are descended from people who came to the area to work on plantations. Some Indian laborers still work alongside David, but he doesn't have much to do with them. As far as he is concerned, they belong to a different class.

At the Roman Catholic boys' school he attends, however, David bumps elbows with friends from several different groups — Indian, Chinese, Malay, and European. Though his schoolmates speak various languages at home, they all speak English in school. By now David understands English as though it were his "first" language — but it isn't. He grew up speaking Tamil, one of the languages of southern India, where he was born.

Like most Indians in Malaysia, David's mother and father cling to the language and ways of the Indian homeland. But they have also adopted many of the Western ways brought to Malaysia by the British. One example occurs at the family breakfast table. In the morning David has eggs, bread and butter, and coffee, as many English people do. But his bread is made of rice flour, and he often eats it with a hot, spicy Indian mixture called curry.

The blend of Indian and English dishes is only one of the ways that David mixes traditional and Western styles. He plays time-honored Indian games — plus tennis and badminton. He visits the homes of Chinese friends to observe their special holidays such as Chinese New Year. As a Christian, he goes to church on Christmas Eve, decorates a tree, and exchanges presents. His life combines many customs and traditions.

So do the lives of a majority of Malaysians. The mixture of peoples and life-styles can be fascinating and appealing. But cultural variety can lead to conflict. That is probably one reason why most Southeast Asians prefer to stick to familiar, traditional ways.

Double-check

Review

1. Who are the *hua-chiao?*

2. What city is the center of trade for Southeast Asia?

3. What does *towkay* mean in Chinese?

4. What country are David's ties to?

5. About how many Indians are there in Malaysia?

Discussion

1. Many Chinese in Southeast Asia still consider themselves sojourners. Do you think they actually try to blend in with the rest of the population? Compare this group with ethnic groups in the U.S. — black, Hispanic, American Indian. Do you think minority groups should "blend in" with a majority culture — or keep their traditions? Why? Is it hard to be part of two cultures? Give reasons for your answers.

2. The man is head of the family in traditional Chinese families. What are some other nations which are considered "patriarchal"? Do you think these societies would be different if women were the heads of the families? Why, or why not?

3. Many Indian women still wear saris. Saris are floor-length and are wrapped around the body. How would this affect the movement and activity of women in their daily lives? How do styles of clothing affect our lives? How are they changing?

Activities

1. Some students might role-play Mr. Wu and his family as sojourners in the U.S. Other students might role-play some American families living in the Wus' neighborhood. In the role-playing, explore these questions: How do you think the Wus would feel about their neighborhood? Do you think they would feel "a part of things"? Or do you think they would keep themselves separate? What would the other families do?

2. Some students might research and report on Indian customs, foods, and traditional holidays. Some could bring in samples of Madras cloth — or an Indian curry dish for the class to taste.

3. A person of Chinese descent might be invited to the classroom to discuss Chinese traditions, values, and culture. Some students might prepare a list of questions for the speaker in advance.

Skills

MALAYSIA'S ETHNIC GROUPS

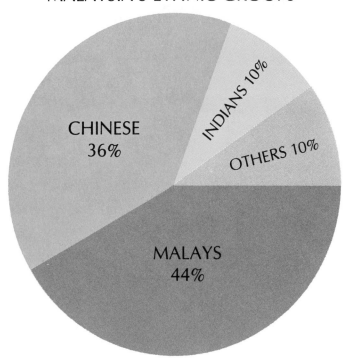

Source: *The 1980 World Almanac*

Use the circle graph above and information in Chapter 8 to answer the following questions.

1. What is the source of the information in this graph?
(a) the text   (b) the Chinese consulate   (c) *The 1980 World Almanac*

2. This chart shows the percentages of groups of people who live in what country?
(a) Malaysia   (b) China   (c) India

3. What is the largest group of people in Malaysia?
(a) Indians   (b) Chinese   (c) Malays

4. A little more than one third of Malaysians are members of what group?
(a) Indians   (b) Chinese   (c) others

5. David Chandy belongs to a group that makes up what percentage of Malaysians?
(a) 10   (b) 36   (c) 44

THE
LAND

Hugging the rim of the world's largest continent, most nations of Southeast Asia are dependent on the water. In the watery world of the island nations, villagers grow rice on hilly terraces to make the most of available land. On the mainland villagers have long used their lakes and rivers as avenues of trade.

BOUNTY: *Almost any tropical plant thrives in Southeast Asia's soil — even the spindly bamboo (right). Two reasons for all the greenery: plenty of rain (above) and rich soil, nourished, on some islands, by ash from nearby volcanoes (below).*

108

USES: Some of Southeast Asia's land serves as sites for growing cities such as Singapore (above). Parts of Indochina have become battlefields of war (lower left). But the most common use of land throughout the area is for raising crops. In Sabah (upper left), as elsewhere, the most common crop is rice.

THE PEOPLE

In spite of recent conflicts, Southeast
Asians live on a historic crossroad
of world trade. They have usually
welcomed outsiders, and sometimes
accepted their ideas. Chinese political
drama has been adapted for audiences
in Vietnam (left). Medical knowledge from
the outside world also helps meet the
needs of Vietnamese (below).

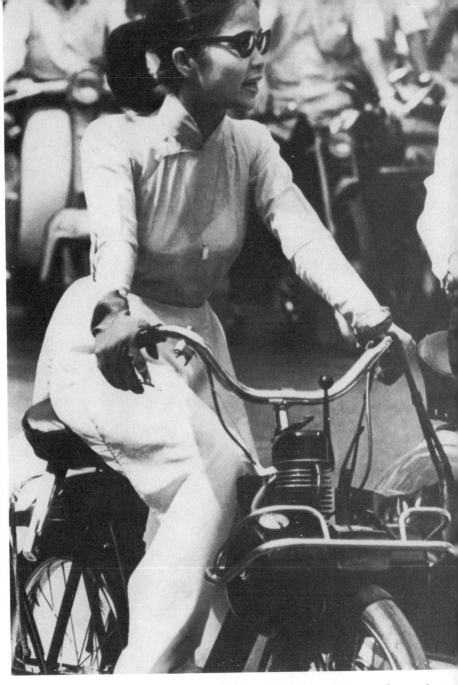

VARIETY: In Southeast Asia the mixture of peoples seems almost endless. Clockwise from top left: an Indonesian girl wearing a local headress, an old man from the Vietnamese hills, a Vietnamese woman riding her motorbike, and a group of Burmese enjoying the annual Water Festival in Rangoon.

HOMEMAKERS: Like people everywhere, Southeast Asians live by rules inherited from the past. In Vietnam, tradition guides the style of cooking (above) and the method of examining grain (below). In Sulawesi, tradition encourages villagers to pitch in on major projects such as moving a house (left).

THE ECONOMY

Though times are changing, Southeast Asia remains long on manpower and short on machines. Even some machine-driven industries continue to rely on people and animals to get things done. Women still stoop in streams to pan tin by hand. Elephants are still used for nosing teak logs onto railroad carts.

FOOD: *Most Southeast Asian diets revolve around one staple food — rice. Growing it takes patience and hard work (right). Once harvested, the crop goes to market (below) where it is sometimes sold along with another staple — fish (above). Clockwise from top left, these scenes are of Cambodia, Vietnam, Sabah.*

ENERGY: In recent years Southeast Asia has been steadily tapping new sources of energy. Study these photos of Singapore harbor (upper right), Bangkok street (lower right), Bangkok typing class (above), and oil field in Brunei (top of page). What "new" sources of energy do they illustrate?

THE CULTURE

Of all the many religions of Southeast Asia, Buddhism has left perhaps the most lasting mark on the landscape. Its relics include the art which decorates the Borobudur temples in central Java (left) and shrines of the ancient Thai capital at Ayutthaya (below).

MOODS: Customs vary as widely as the people who observe them. Rituals may be sorrowful as an Indochinese funeral (below) or as spiritual as a Singapore ceremony involving a Hindu needle tree (left). Some rituals are even meant to be comic. An example is the Balinese takeoff on a war dance at right.

PATTERNS: Southeast Asia's arts reflect the values of its people. Styles tend to be subtle and to show attention to details. Left: rice barn in Sulawesi. Above, pattern on an Indonesian batik. Top right, statues of spirits said to be keepers of the Shwe Dagon Pagoda in Burma. Right, figures from an Indonesian puppet show known as a shadow play.

3
VOYAGES
THROUGH
TIME

Chapter 9

Lost Empires

THE CAMBODIAN CITY OF ANGKOR has a touch of mystery. It lies tucked away in the depths of the jungle like a jewel kept under lock and key. Its weather-beaten walls wrap the inner city in a cloak of secrecy. Its green-gray towers peep above the tree-tops in half-hidden tribute to the past.

Today Angkor is almost a ghost town. But centuries ago it was the center of a thriving empire. It was the home of the Khmers, who had settled in the area since prehistoric times. At the end of the ninth century A.D., they built Angkor as a sacred city which included the royal palaces and temples of their "god-kings."

Today Angkor is a lasting monument to its ancient builders. One of its special wonders is its artwork. Along the temple walls are thousands of feet of sculpture showing fierce battles, hunting scenes, and ceremonial dances. Everywhere are statues — of lions, snakes, and Hindu gods.

If the buildings of Angkor are aged, so is the history they represent. To put Angkor in clearer focus, it is necessary to look at it as part of the entire Southeast Asian past. And that takes us back long before Angkor was built.

Perhaps the first large-scale migration to Southeast Asia was the one made by the Malay people. This migration must have taken place many thousands of years ago — no one knows just when. Following the Malays came a variety of different people, also moving south. They included the Khmers, who settled Cambodia, and the Viets, who settled Vietnam.

In many parts of Southeast Asia, this long series of migrations meant centuries of steady development. One cultural layer was piled on top of another. The culture of the area was also affected by those who simply visited it. The most frequent visitors became Indian merchants, who began making regular voyages to the area about the time of Christ.

Their voyages were made possible by the seasonal nature of the winds that blow in the Indian Ocean and southern Asia. From April to October, the summer monsoon, heavy with ocean moisture, blows steadily out of the southwest. This summer monsoon carried the merchant vessels from India's east coast to the Southeast Asian markets. In the fall the winds change direction — the dry winter monsoon blows out of the northeast. Riding these autumn winds, the traders sailed home.

The reason for this shuttling back and forth was trade. Indian merchants carried on their business in Malaya, on Java, and on the Molucca* Islands of the Indonesian chain. They brought glass from Venice, cloth from Cairo, and other items. They sold these items for spices and ebony, bird feathers from the Banda Islands, and gold from Borneo and Sumatra.

Migrations from CHINA and INDIA

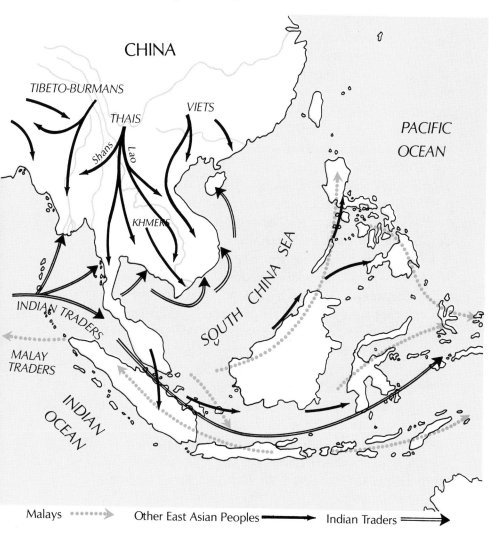

The map above indicates where some Southeast
Asian groups originated. The Thais, Viets,
and Tibeto-Burmans all moved south from the
north-central part of East Asia at various
stages in the past. Experts still dispute the
origins of Malay people. But their migrations
are believed to have taken place 4,000 to 5,000
years ago and perhaps even earlier than that.

In time, some of the Indian merchants settled in Southeast Asia, building new communities similar to the ones they had left behind. With them they brought two of their religions, Hinduism and Buddhism. They also brought many of the values and customs of the Indian way of life.

The Indians gradually gained the respect of many Southeast Asians. As this respect widened, a number of Indian-style kingdoms came into being among people who were not Indians themselves. The most powerful of these kingdoms was that of the Khmers. At its peak it extended across all of present-day Cambodia and parts of Vietnam, Laos, and Thailand.

The Khmers are a mystery to scholars. Nearly all written traces of their civilization — their books and other documents — have been lost. The only written records that remain are their own inscriptions carved in the stone walls of temples and brief accounts given in Chinese histories. But these speak mainly of religion or list the names of cities, states, and kings. They tell little of what happened in the old days.

Thus, scholars can only guess at the origins of this group. One guess is that the Khmers are one of several distantly related tribes which may have lived originally in southern China. According to this theory, these tribes all pushed into Burma, Thailand, and Vietnam at some time in the unknown past. The Khmers built their kingdom of Angkor around A.D. 800. For about six centuries thereafter, they dominated most of Indochina and parts of Thailand.

Few "on-the-spot" accounts of the Khmer empire have survived the centuries. One that has was written by Chou Ta-Kouan,* a Chinese diplomat who visited Angkor in 1295. Chou told of the amazing size and wealth of Angkor. He left a vivid description of the layout of the city:

Sculpture carved in the stone wall of a pavilion at Angkor shows the ancient Khmers in the thick of battle. Study the artwork carefully. What clues does it offer about the Khmers and the way they must have lived?

"Outside the walls is a large moat; outside the moat there are large bridges with roads coming in. On each side of the bridges [there are] 54 stone divinities [gods] which have the appearance of 'stone generals'; they are gigantic and terrible.... The parapets [railings] on the bridges are entirely carved in stone, in the form of serpents which all have nine heads. The 54 divinities all hang onto the serpents with their hands and look as though they are trying to stop them from running away."

Much of this art was religious in nature. So, in fact, were many of Angkor's buildings. As Hindus, the city's builders believed their kings became gods after death. As a result, they put up temples as burial places for their god-kings. The largest of these

◄§ As Hindus, Khmers believed
their kings became gods after
death. Thus they put up temples
as burial places for their god-kings.

temples was known as Angkor Wat. It contained stones, some weighing six tons, which came from quarries 25 or more miles away.

By the time that Chou arrived in Angkor, however, the city had been transformed from a Hindu center to a Buddhist one. Chou described Buddhist monks who "shave their heads, wear yellow robes,...and go barefoot." The Khmer king was rich and powerful. He wore "around his neck...almost three pounds of pearls. On his wrists, ankles, and fingers, he has bracelets and rings of gold encrusted with cat's eyes."

The king traveled about with a long train of followers. "The ministers and princes are all riding elephants; in front of them one sees from afar their red parasols [sun shades], which are innumerable. After them arrive the wives...of the king...; they have certainly more than a hundred parasols flecked with gold."

At last came the king himself, "standing on an elephant and holding in his hand the precious sword," symbol of his royal authority. The tusks of the king's elephants "are also in a sheath of gold.... Many elephants press all about him and again there are troops to protect him."

The scene showed signs of power and glory. But even as Chou was visiting the city, Angkor's power was declining. In the 1200's warlike Thais from China had begun expanding toward the Khmers. The Thais and the Khmers fought on and off for about

Buffalo idle among the water lilies in the moat which surrounds the temple of Angkor Wat.

200 years. By the 15th century, the kings of Angkor had been forced to leave it and establish their capital farther south and east. Although they were later able to return to Angkor, it never regained its earlier glory.

Meanwhile, the center of Southeast Asian trade was also shifting southward. In the early 15th century it came to rest in a sleepy, sun-seared city on the Malay Peninsula. This was Malacca, which stood guard over a vital shipping channel known as the Straits of Malacca.

Along the city's narrow streets and alleyways, merchants swapped a dizzying array of merchandise. Into Malacca came expensive silks and satins from China, gold from Sumatra, tin from Malaya, and teak from the forests of Burma. Above all, there were nutmeg, pepper, and cloves from the Spice Islands.

The men who managed most of the buying and selling were merchants from the west coast of India. Though local Malayans ruled the city, these Indian merchants held the power behind the throne. It was they who helped introduce yet another religion to the area — Islam (see Chapter 13). Before long, Malacca had become a leading center of Islamic culture.

At first most of those who carried on their business in Malacca came from China, India, or Java. But as time went on, the city began to attract travelers from farther away. By the middle of the 15th century, Arab, Persian, and Turkish traders were sailing to Malacca. Through their travels Asian goods found their way to European shores.

These long-distance voyagers gave an extra spur to Southeast Asian commerce. But unfortunately they also posed a special threat. Foreign trade could easily lead to foreign control. Over the next few centuries Asians would learn how serious a threat that could be.

Chapter 10

Merchants and Conquerors

ONCE MERCHANTS FROM the Middle East had opened up trading links with Southeast Asia, others were bound to follow. And European merchants soon did just that.

The first of them to record his visit to the region was Marco Polo of Venice. He stopped off in Sumatra in 1290 during a homeward journey from China. He later described Sumatra as filled with "merchants who buy and sell costly goods from which they reap great profit." It was an island rich in "all the precious spices that can be found in the world."

In Marco Polo's time, "great profit" and "precious spices" usually went hand in hand. Such items as pepper, cloves, and cinnamon had an importance which they mostly lack today. In the days before refrigerators, untreated meat soon took on a foul taste and smell. Only spices could make such meat tasty enough to eat. So it was the spice trade which first lured Europeans to the islands of Southeast Asia.

Two centuries after Marco Polo's journey,

✨ By the turn of the century, the French had taken possession of all Indochina.

European explorers began to open up a trade route to the Orient by sea. One of them became famous by never making it. Christopher Columbus, thinking that the world was round, figured that he could reach the Molucca Islands of the Indonesian chain by sailing west from Spain. Though he was right about the world's shape, he underestimated its size. In 1498, in his third Atlantic voyage, he sailed west and stumbled upon a whole new continent.

Columbus was not the only European sailor trying to reach the East Indies. The Portuguese sent ship after ship down the west coast of Africa to find a way of sailing around the continent. Countless ships were lost in the treacherous waters off Africa's coast. But finally, in 1498, Vasco da Gama* rounded the continent's southern tip. Then he sailed north to Goa* on the southwest coast of India.

Although da Gama stopped short of Southeast Asia, he came much closer than any European sailor of his day. At Goa he loaded his ships with goods from all of East Asia. He and his crew returned to Portugal with enough spices to pay for the cost of the journey 60 times over. To no one's surprise, other Portuguese sailors soon returned to the area for more.

In 1511 the Portuguese seized Malacca, the seaport on the Straits of Malacca (see Chapter 9). For a century thereafter, the Portuguese controlled the trade in pepper, cloves, and cinnamon. These spices fetched enormous prices in the markets of

Vietnamese painting shows French troops taking a fort in their conquest of Vietnam. Can you identify the French and the Vietnamese?

Europe. Spices became so valuable that a king of Portugal gave his daughter a dowry, not in gold or jewels, but pepper, when she married a king of Spain.

Spain was also pushing ahead with its contacts in Southeast Asia. In 1521 Ferdinand Magellan* sailed around the southernmost point of South America and reached the Pacific island of Cebu,* claiming it for Spain. These and other nearby islands were then renamed the Philippines after the man who became King Philip II of Spain.

But claiming a colony and controlling it were two different things. The Spanish did not begin to take full control of the Philippines for almost 50 years. When they did, their aim was not only to win trade but also to promote their Roman Catholic faith. To achieve the second purpose, the Spanish sent out missionaries, who slowly managed to convert many Filipinos.

Still later in the same century, other European nations arrived in Southeast Asia. In 1599 English merchants started their own East India Company to foster trade with the region. But the biggest threat to the Portuguese came from the Dutch. The first Dutch trading ships appeared in the islands of Indonesia in 1596. A few years later the Dutch government chartered the United Dutch East India Company to handle all its trade with Asia.

This brought the Dutch into direct conflict with the Portuguese, who claimed exclusive control of the spice business. The Dutch and the Portuguese went to war, and the Dutch won many battles. In 1641, after several tries, they seized Malacca from the Portuguese.

In winning control over large portions of Southeast Asia, the Dutch found themselves in trouble with the Southeast Asians themselves. It seemed to many of

Colonialism in *SOUTHEAST ASIA*, 1939

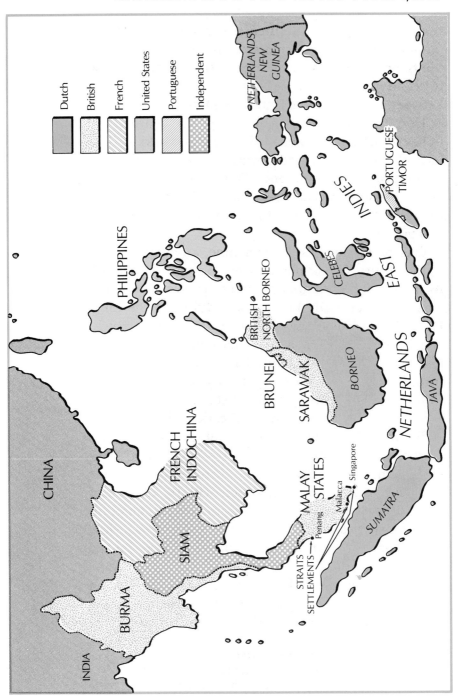

Dutch
British
French
United States
Portuguese
Independent

NETHERLANDS NEW GUINEA

PORTUGUESE TIMOR

PHILIPPINES

INDIES

CELEBES

EAST

BRITISH NORTH BORNEO

BRUNEI

SARAWAK

BORNEO

NETHERLANDS

JAVA

FRENCH INDOCHINA

CHINA

SIAM

MALAY STATES

Singapore

SUMATRA

Malacca

Penang

STRAITS SETTLEMENTS

BURMA

INDIA

these people that the Dutch had come in search of plunder. Indonesian farmers resented being made to sell their spices, coffee, and rice to the Dutch at a low price. This resulted in endless armed disputes between the Indonesians and the Dutch.

Despite this fighting, some Europeans regarded the riches of the East Indies as theirs for the asking. The lure of the spice trade attracted many European adventurers to the scene. Some became traders; others became mercenaries (hired soldiers) for local rulers. A few even tried to carve out kingdoms for themselves.

One of the luckiest — for a time, anyway — was a 17th-century Greek named Constantine Phaulkon.* As a teenager, Phaulkon found his way to Siam, where he eventually became an adviser to the king. He built a splendid palace, kept English bodyguards, and lived like a prince. Still not content, Phaulkon laid plans for making himself master of the country through the rule of a puppet king. But in the end Phaulkon's enemies got the better of him. They tried him for treason, and beheaded him.

Phaulkon's schemes were about as close as any European ever came to controlling Siam. But elsewhere in Southeast Asia, Europeans were far more successful at imposing their will. By the end of the 18th century, the Spanish were firmly planted in the Philippines, and the Dutch, in Indonesia. Now still other European nations took their places on the scene.

From ports along the coast of India, the British sent sailing ships heading eastward in search of trade with China. The ships often faced threats from

Japanese print of Indonesian life shows an 18th-century Dutch merchant and his Javanese servant walking a dog. Both wear coats made of batik.

monsoon winds or the vessels of unfriendly nations. One way to protect the ships was to find or create some safe harbors along the way.

With this in mind, a British governor named Thomas Stamford Raffles took possession of the tiny fishing colony of Singapore in 1819. There he set up a British trading station and began building what would soon become Southeast Asia's major port. Seven years later the British gained control of Malacca from the Dutch through a treaty. Then they combined three ports — Singapore, Malacca, and the island of Penang* farther north — into the colony of the Straits Settlements.

Next colonialism moved north. From India, Britain fanned out into Burma, making it a province of the British empire in 1886. In 1884 France grabbed the northern section of present-day Vietnam. By the turn of the century, the French had taken possession of all Indochina.

Now most of Southeast Asia had fallen under the European thumb. In many ways Europeans turned out to be as bold in their colony-building as they had been in their explorations. The French brought rubber trees to Vietnam, and the Dutch planted coffee trees in Indonesia. In addition, Europeans built schools and roads — even, in some cases, entire industries.

But the European influence did not go very deep. The Europeans did not socialize much with the Southeast Asians. Most settled in market towns and seaports and confined themselves to commerce. Only rarely did Europeans move out to the countryside where a majority of Asians lived. Thus, a barrier was raised to close contact between East and West.

The major exception to all this took place in the Philippines. There Spanish missionaries ventured into the countryside to work among the people. As a result, most Filipinos gradually adopted the Roman Catholic religion and Spanish customs in music and dress. Control of the Philippines passed to the United States at the close of the Spanish-American War in 1898. But so strong was the Spanish influence that it still lingers today.

In other parts of Southeast Asia, however, European culture had much less impact. Even the term "colonial power" is misleading as applied to Southeast Asia, for it implies that Europeans went there in huge numbers. No more than about 300,000 Europeans, many of mixed descent, ever lived in the area at any one time. If any nation was colonizing the region, it was China. At least 30 times more Chinese than Europeans were living there by the close of the colonial period.

Not until well into the 20th century did European culture really take root. Even then it was usually limited to the larger towns and cities. The Vietnamese city of Hanoi, for example, blossomed with many signs of French influence — broad boulevards, public parks, sidewalk cafés. But out in the countryside the peasants continued to live as their forefathers had for generations.

And so Western influences varied widely from country to country and community to community. Nonetheless, Europeans did introduce one idea that soon became popular throughout the region. It was the concept of self-government — the belief that every group of people has the right to govern itself.

Many Asians were quick to ask why the idea should not be applied to themselves. They began to call for independence from colonial rule. The idea of self-government became the Europeans' own undoing in Southeast Asia.

Double-check

Review

1. What city was the home of the Khmers?

2. Who made perhaps the first large-scale migration to Southeast Asia?

3. What was the most powerful Indian-style kingdom in Southeast Asia?

4. Who was the first European merchant to record his visit to Southeast Asia?

5. Whom were the Philippines named after?

Discussion

1. What countries used to be some of the biggest colonial powers in the world? What countries are now? The U.S. and the U.S.S.R. have been exploring the moon. Should the moon be colonized? Why, or why not? If so, how?

2. The spices that were considered "riches" by explorers and traders in the past are not so important today. What kinds of resources are? How are the countries that have such commodities affected when their resources become valuable? Give examples to support your answers.

3. The European culture took hold only in the cities of Southeast Asia, while the people in the countryside continued to live the way they always had. Why would the cities be more likely to accept "foreign ways"? Is this true of cities in the United States? What are some advantages of foreign influences coming to a city? What are some disadvantages?

Activities

1. The class might visit a museum or gallery that contains examples of Asian culture or art. If this is not possible, a scholar from a nearby university might be invited to speak to the class about Southeast Asian religious and cultural history.

2. Some students might research and report on the explorers of Southeast Asia — their lives, what their discoveries were, their problems. The routes of their journeys could be traced on a large wall map.

3. Some students might bring in samples of spices that originated in Southeast Asia. Other students might bring in foods that are prepared with these spices.

Skills

Use the maps and other information in Chapters 9 and 10 to answer the following questions.

1. On their way to Southeast Asian lands, the Indian traders did *not* sail in which body of water?
(a) Indian Ocean   (b) Pacific Ocean   (c) South China Sea

2. Of the following peoples, which group is most likely to have visited India?
(a) Viets   (b) Thais   (c) Malays

3. In 1939 which Southeast Asian country was independent?
(a) Burma   (b) Siam   (c) Brunei

4. In 1939 who controlled the Southeast Asian country named after a Spanish king?
(a) Netherlands   (b) Portugal   (c) United States

Chapter 11

Europe Takes Its Leave

EXCEPT PERHAPS IN THE PHILIPPINES, colonial rule meant little to most villagers of Southeast Asia. It rarely touched their customs, and it rarely changed their lives. From year to year, from decade to decade, these villagers continued to live much as their ancestors had lived before colonialism.

Then, in the early 1940's, a bomb burst into this region that time had almost forgotten.

It began with a rumble of guns on a distant frontier. In 1939 World War II broke out in Europe, drawing several nations into a desperate fight for freedom. By 1941 Nazi Germany had already overrun France and the Netherlands, and Britain was fighting for its survival. These countries could no longer send forces to protect their colonies in Southeast Asia. Left unprotected, the colonies became plums ripe for the picking by another ambitious world power.

In 1941 Imperial Japan entered the war on the side of Germany. Japan's aim was to destroy the old colonial empire and conquer Southeast Asia for itself. But first it had to overcome the armed might of the United States. On December 7, 1941, the Japanese struck without warning against the U.S. naval base at Pearl Harbor, Hawaii. They sank or badly damaged much of the U.S. Pacific fleet.

Now the way was clear for a Japanese advance. In the following months the Japanese quickly overran almost all of Southeast Asia. The small French military posts in Indochina put up no resistance. Elsewhere in the area the British and Dutch tried to halt the Japanese but failed. The great British naval base at Singapore fell before it could prepare its defense.

At first the people of the region welcomed the Japanese as fellow Asians who might lead them to independence. But the Japanese had no such plan. Instead, they wanted to exploit the area's riches — its tin, oil, rubber, rice. No less than the Europeans, the Japanese hoped to turn these riches to their own benefit.

Among Southeast Asians, however, the hope for independence kept right on growing. Fanning this hope were nationalists (people who wanted their countries free from any kind of foreign rule and who were willing to fight to get their way). Across the mountains and jungles of Southeast Asia, nationalists formed small bands of hit-and-run fighters known as guerrillas.* Then, using homemade weapons or guns stolen from the enemy, the guerrillas set out to do battle with the Japanese.

In Vietnam, Burma, and Malaya, many guerrilla bands were led by Communists. Once Japan could be defeated, the Communists were determined to take over and run their countries as Communist states.

By early 1945 it was clear that Japan was, in fact, going down to defeat. U.S. forces were hopping from island to island across the Pacific, drawing ever nearer to the home islands of Japan. In a last-ditch effort to save what they could from the war, the Japanese encouraged Southeast Asians to set up their own "independent" governments. Japan wanted to deny the Europeans a chance to regain their colonies after the war's end.

In this Japan succeeded. It surrendered to the U.S. and its allies on August 14, 1945. But when the British, French, and Dutch returned to Southeast Asia to take back their old holdings, they ran into opposition. Cries for independence were echoing through the region. And this time the cries would not be stilled.

Nationalist movements got further support in the late 1940's when two nations of the area were given their independence. The U.S. granted it to the Philippines in 1946, and the British, to Burma two years later. These developments increased the sense of impatience in other Southeast Asian countries. In some areas nationalists turned to waging guerrilla warfare against their European rulers.

No war is pleasant, but to many people a guerrilla war seems especially cruel. It involves both sides in a deadly game of hide-and-seek. Out in the countryside, the guerrilla fighter mixes in among the peasants so that no one knows who is friend and who is foe. Often he strikes from remote mountain and jungle hideouts, hitting his enemies at their weakest point and then fading away.

Fireworks lit up the Manila sky on July 4, 1946, the day Filipinos proclaimed independence from the U.S. What is the significance of the date?

The successful guerrilla fighter often wages two different kinds of campaigns at the same time. One is a campaign to build popular support. He tells the peasants that the existing government is their enemy. He tries to convince the mass of the people to join his side.

The other campaign is one of fear. Its methods include the use of terror — the village official suddenly kidnapped in the dead of night; the policeman suddenly killed by an exploding grenade. With such tactics, the guerrilla hopes to weaken the power and authority of the existing government among the people. Once the government has been weakened, it is likelier to fall.

Southeast Asia offered an almost perfect setting for the success of guerrilla warfare. The deep forests and jungles offered concealment for guerrilla fighters. The widely scattered population made it easier for guerrillas to win support. What was most important, a growing number of Southeast Asians were getting weary of rule by foreigners. Some were ready to back independence movements, even if Communist-led.

In Vietnam the struggle against the French was directed by a man who called himself Ho Chi Minh.* He was an ardent nationalist and an equally ardent Communist. At first Ho tried to persuade the French to withdraw peacefully from Indochina. The French refused. So Ho and the Communists launched a campaign to force them out.

The battle raged for eight years and cost thousands upon thousands of lives. Ho was a master of guerrilla tactics, and gradually his forces gained the upper hand. Finally, the Vietnamese Communists gained a decisive victory. They surrounded and crushed the French stronghold of Dien Bien Phu* far in the north.

◄§ Across the mountains and jungles of Southeast Asia, nationalists formed small bands of hit-and-run fighters known as guerrillas.

The French had been beaten, but Ho's victory was not complete. At a peace conference in Geneva, Switzerland, in 1954, Vietnam was temporarily split into two parts. The north would be ruled by Ho and the Communists. The south would be turned over to non-Communist Vietnamese, friendlier to Europe and the United States. According to the plan, elections would later be held to reunite the country.

While all of this was going on, the British were having similar troubles in Malaya. There Communists had also started a guerrilla movement, made up mostly of people of Chinese descent. But the native Malays had often resented the wealthy and powerful Chinese living among them, and they were willing to work with the British to defeat the guerrillas. In the early 1950's they managed to crush the guerrilla movement. Then, in 1957, Malaya became independent with British blessings.

In both Malaya and Vietnam, guerrilla forces were led by Communists. In the largest country of the area, Indonesia, the situation was quite different. There the movement for independence was *not* led by Communists. It was led by people who had worked with the Japanese during the war in the hope of obtaining independence.

When the war with Japan ended, the Dutch tried to resume their control in Indonesia. But soon the Dutch became embroiled in a bitter war with Indonesian nationalists led by an engineer named Sukarno.* Sukarno and his followers fought the

Dutch until 1949. Then the Dutch gave up under pressure from the United Nations, and Indonesia became an independent republic with Sukarno as its president.

By 1960 nearly all of Southeast Asia was free of foreign rule. Only the British and the Portuguese held any territory at all. In 1963 two of the remaining British holdings—the island of Singapore and certain areas in northern Borneo—were joined to form the Federation of Malaysia (see page 52). Singapore later separated from the federation in 1965. Britain controlled the oil-rich protectorate of Brunei in northern Borneo until the end of 1983 when it was granted complete independence. Portugal occupied the eastern part of the island of Timor until 1976, when Indonesia invaded and annexed it.

The departure of the Europeans left Southeast Asians to manage their own affairs. But it did not necessarily bring a new and better life. Nor did it erase all signs of the colonial past. Several great powers — the U.S., the Soviet Union, and China — still exerted their influence within Southeast Asia. And in some parts of the region new conflicts were already darkening the horizon like thunderclouds before a storm.

In the 1940's and 1950's, the two men pictured on the opposite page led their separate Southeast Asian nations to independence. Indonesia's spellbinding Sukarno (top) helped end Dutch rule in his island nation. Vietnam's Ho Chi Minh (bottom) roused his countrymen to drive out the French.

Double-check

Review

1. What happened in Europe in 1939?

2. What country's aim was to destroy the old colonial empire and conquer Southeast Asia for itself?

3. What are guerrillas?

4. Who was Ho Chi Minh?

5. What happened to Vietnam in 1954?

Discussion

1. How is guerrilla warfare different from other kinds of warfare? What would be important in this kind of fighting? In what kinds of situations is guerrilla fighting more effective than conventional fighting?

2. Ho Chi Minh led the Vietnamese fight for independence against the French. Do you think the situation in Vietnam would be different today if the French had left peacefully? Give reasons to support your answer. Was the Geneva plan a good solution? Why, or why not? If not, what do you think would have been a good solution?

3. What are some of the ways nations have gained their independence? Does independence solve all their problems? Why, or why not? What new problems might arise when nations gain their independence?

Activities

1. A group of students might research and report on major events in the Pacific region during World War II, with special attention to Southeast Asia. Afterward, a person in your community who was in combat in the Pacific during World War II might be invited to the class to talk about his experiences.

2. Some students might draw political cartoons depicting the spread of independence throughout Southeast Asian countries; the departure of the Europeans; the continued influence of the U.S., the Soviet Union, and China; or the new conflicts darkening the horizon.

3. Some students might pretend to be Ho Chi Minh or Sukarno, writing his last diary entries about his life and about what he thinks will happen to his country after he dies.

Skills

EUROPE TAKES ITS LEAVE

1939

1941

1945

1946

1948

1949

1954

1957

1963

A. Japan surrenders to the U.S.

B. Indonesia becomes independent.

C. Japan enters the war.

D. Burma becomes independent.

E. Singapore joins the Federation of Malaysia.

F. A peace conference is held in Geneva.

G. The Philippines become independent.

H. Malaya becomes independent.

I. World War II begins.

Use the events listed above and information in Chapter 11 to do the following things on a separate sheet of paper. Write the years down the left side of the paper. Then write the letter of each event next to the year in which it happened. (The events are not in the correct order in the list above.)

4
VALUES
AND
TRADITIONS

Chapter 12

Buddhas, Bonzes, and Pagodas

MILE FOR MILE, Southeast Asia probably has a greater variety of religions than any other single area in the world. In many places, five major faiths and a number of smaller ones exist side by side. The major faiths all began outside Southeast Asia but have put down firm roots there over the years. From India came Buddhism and Hinduism. From the Middle East came Islam. Confucianism began in China. And the West brought Christianity.

Because of all this variety, Southeast Asians tend to be tolerant of other people's faiths. Some of them even combine two or more religions in their own form of worship. Thus, a Burmese may be both a Buddhist and a follower of Confucius. Or an Indonesian may be a Moslem, yet also follow ancient Hindu beliefs and rituals.

Even so, most Southeast Asians do consider themselves to be followers of one definite religion.

Which religion this is depends partly on where in Southeast Asia they live. Many island people are Moslems (see Chapter 13). In the countries of the mainland, however, most people are Buddhists — more than 70 million in all.

☆ ☆ ☆ ☆ ☆ ☆ ☆ ☆ ☆

Buddhism was founded by an Indian prince named Siddhartha Gautama.* He was born in the foothills of the Himalayas about 2,500 years ago. Little is known for certain about his life. But this is the story that has come down over the centuries:

One day Gautama left his palace, his wealth, his beautiful wife, and his small son, and took up the life of a wandering holy man. He spent many years in study and poverty. Finally, he discovered what he believed to be the truth. It came to him while meditating for 49 days beneath a fig tree in India.

Gautama taught his followers the Four Truths: (1) Suffering comes to everyone, everywhere, at all times. (2) Suffering is caused by selfish desires for power, wealth, and pleasure. (3) The way to free oneself from suffering is to give up selfish desires. (4) The way to do this is to follow the Middle Path.

Gautama chose this name because the Middle Path avoids two extremes — too much pleasure and too much worry about life. To find this path a person must think, speak, and act rightly. He must avoid killing any living thing. He must not steal, lie, get drunk, or slip into any other immoral acts.

Gautama came to be known as Lord Buddha — the Enlightened One. His Four Truths made up the core of Buddhism. Missionaries from Ceylon (now Sri Lanka) and India carried Buddhism to the people of Southeast Asia. There, the new religion gradually blended in with the earlier beliefs of the people. Over

160

SOUTHEAST ASIAN RELIGIONS

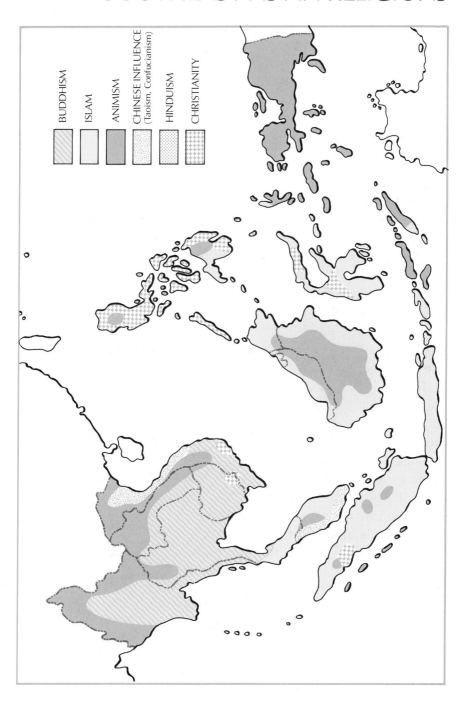

BUDDHISM

ISLAM

ANIMISM

CHINESE INFLUENCE
(Taoism, Confucianism)

HINDUISM

CHRISTIANITY

✑ Buddhists believe that donations to monks help the giver.

the centuries it also split into different branches in much the same way that Christianity is divided into different churches.

No matter what its form, Buddhism has always had a deep influence on the way its followers live and think. You can get some idea of this influence from the immense number of pagodas (temples) and statues of the Lord Buddha that are found throughout the Buddhist countries of Southeast Asia.

You can also see the influence of Buddhism on the crowded streets of Southeast Asian cities. Along these streets yellow-robed Buddhist monks mingle with the ordinary people. Monks are quite numerous throughout Buddhist lands. In Thailand alone there are some 150,000 of them and 20,000 monasteries.

Every year tens of thousands of young men leave their homes and jobs to spend some time in the monasteries as novice (beginning) monks. This ancient practice is followed by people from all walks of life in Buddhist countries. Even the kings of Thailand serve as novices, and one Thai king spent 26 years as a monk before he took the throne.

A Buddhist monk is called a *bonze.** Monks promise to lead a life of poverty, humility, study, and purity, like the Lord Buddha himself. How does this work in practice? Consider the experiences of Maung Hla, the Burmese boy from a village on the banks of the Irrawaddy River (*see* Chapter 6).

Like other Burmese boys, Hla spent several months in a monastery as a novice (see page 74).

Just after dawn, a Thai boy places rice in a Buddhist monk's begging bowl.

Some boys stay on for years, perhaps for life, and become regular monks. But Hla lived as a novice for only a few months — long enough to learn about his religion and its values. Then, lonely and homesick, he returned to his village.

On entering the monastery, Hla shaved his head and put on yellow robes. His only possessions as a monk were three pieces of cloth for his robes, a begging bowl, a mat to sleep on, an umbrella to shade him from the heat of the sun, and a needle and thread to repair his clothes. He also had a water strainer to make sure that he did not swallow, even by accident, a living insect.

Buddhists believe it is wrong to kill any creature, even a tiny insect. They think of all living things as belonging to one big family of life. They also believe that living things are born over and over again. If a man does not lead a good life, he may be reborn as an animal. So, to a Buddhist, killing an animal is very much like killing a human being.

Like all Buddhist monks, Hla had a long and carefully planned day. At four A.M. he was awakened by the ringing of a bell. It was the signal to rise and take part in the first of the daily ceremonies, lighting candles at an altar before an image of Buddha.

Then, walking in pairs, the monks told each other how they had broken the Buddhist rules of conduct since their last confession. After this, the monks and novices returned to their quarters to rest for a while.

At sunrise, the monks took their begging bowls and walked to nearby communities. Buddhist law forbids them to ask people directly for food or money, nor can they thank the givers. Buddhists believe that donations to monks help the giver and improve his status when he dies and is born again. So it is the givers, not the monks, who should be grateful.

Buddhism says that people are born over and over until they are purified of all sins and desires. Then they enter perfect spiritual happiness called *nirvana.* *

After begging for a time, Hla and the other monks returned to the monastery for breakfast. Then they took part in various rituals, such as chanting and reciting passages from Buddhist scriptures. Before noon, Hla had his big meal of the day. Buddhist monks are not allowed to eat after midday.

In the afternoon, Hla rested for a time and studied the holy books. Then he gathered again in the evening with other bonzes for further religious ceremonies. Once more the bonzes chanted prayers and confessed any violations of the rules of conduct.

About 10 P.M. Hla retired to his dormitory. Just before going to sleep he bowed before an image of the Buddha, recited passages from the scriptures, and thought deeply about the Buddha's teachings.

There are several ranks of Buddhist monks. Higher ranks are reached by spending many years in a monastery and following a regular course of study. But monks are allowed to drop out of the religious life and return to the outside world any time they wish. Some monks stay their whole lives in the monastery. Others stay for shorter periods, then go back to their family and business ties.

As monks, however, they are honored for leading lives like that of the Lord Buddha. Monks play an important role as teachers, instructing people how to read and stressing the right conduct that people should follow. They also take a leading part in the religious festivals and public rituals.

In Southeast Asia, few people can hope to gain great material wealth or fine possessions. But those who follow the Buddhist faith believe that they are richly blessed indeed with spiritual wealth.

Chapter 13

The Message from Mecca

WHAT PART OF THE WORLD do you associate with Islam, the religion of the Moslems? And what kind of people do you first think of as its followers?

Most Westerners would probably answer "the Middle East" and "the Arabs." Yet the world's most populous Moslem nation is *not* in the Middle East and its people are *not* Arabs. As you can guess, this nation is in Southeast Asia. It is Indonesia, which has 130 million Moslems — about one fifth of the world's total.

Of course, you would not be wrong to link Islam with the Middle East. That's where the Moslems' holy city stands — Mecca, in Saudi Arabia. It was on the Arabian Peninsula that men and women first spoke the Arabic language and developed the Arab way of life. And it was there, nearly 1,400 years ago, that the Moslem religion began.

It started with the teachings of an Arab named Mohammed,* born in Mecca in about A.D. 570. In Mohammed's day the Arabs worshiped many spirits and idols. However, there were Jews and Christians

166

living in Arabia, and Mohammed took an interest in their religions. When he was 40, he went off on his own to think about the meaning of life. Then Mohammed began to hear the voice of God explaining how mankind should live and telling him to spread the message.

At first, Mohammed had little success with his preaching. In fact, the people of Mecca made life so miserable for him that he left the city. But gradually Mohammed gathered more followers. Then he came back to Mecca with an army, conquered it, and made it the central city of his religion.

Mohammed did not think of himself as creating a new religion. He believed that God had also given His message to Abraham, Moses, and Jesus — but that men had twisted it away from the truth over the centuries. Now God had spoken to Mohammed to set the record straight for all time.

The basic beliefs of Islam are clear and simple. They are set out in a holy book called the Koran,* which is said to record the words God spoke to Mohammed. Moslems believe that there is only One God, known as Allah, and that Mohammed is His Messenger. They believe that people should lead good lives and that those who do will go to heaven.

The name "Islam" comes from the Koran itself. It is an Arabic word meaning "submission" — since a follower submits to the will of God. "Moslem" is an Arabic word meaning "one who submits." Nearly all Islamic words are from the Arabic language.

At first, as Islam spread through the Middle East, it remained a religion of the Arab peoples. But the Arabs were great traders and travelers, and they spread their religion wherever they went. Some traveled west into North Africa and then south across the Sahara. Others went east, sailing around the coast of India. About A.D. 1300 Islam began to spread through the Malay Peninsula and the Indonesian islands. These are the areas of Southeast Asia which remain Moslem today.

In addition to Indonesia, a majority of the population of Malaysia is Moslem. There are also large numbers of Moslems living in the southern parts of Burma and Thailand which are on the Malay Peninsula. And there are Moslems in the south of the Philippines, on the islands closest to Indonesia.

The Moslems of Southeast Asia have adapted the teachings of Mohammed to fit their own traditions. One example is the role of women. In the Arab society of Mohammed's time, women had practically no rights at all, and many men had a large number of wives. Mohammed tried to improve things for women — but he could not do it all at once. Thus he said that a man could have as many as four wives. Also, Islamic law allows a husband to divorce a wife, but not the other way around.

In Indonesia centuries ago, women had more status than in many parts of the world. It was uncommon for Indonesian men to take more than one wife. The arrival of Islam did not change things much. As for divorce, wives as well as husbands can obtain one in Indonesia.

The roles of women are not the only difference between Islam in Indonesia and Islam in the Middle East. In many respects, Indonesian Moslems lead very different lives from Moslems in other parts of the world. Take Nawi,* age 16, for example. He lives in the big city of Surabaja* in eastern Java.

At noon every Friday Nawi goes with his father to the neighborhood mosque, the Moslem place of worship. Friday is the Moslem holy day, like

Malaysian Moslems kneel facing west — toward Mecca.

Moslems pray five times a day, the first time at dawn and the last time at sunset.

Saturday for Jews and Sunday for Christians. The religious service begins with prayers. Along with the other worshipers, Nawi kneels down facing west — the direction of Mecca. After prayers, one of the elders of the mosque gives a sermon.

Nawi is proud to be a Moslem. But going to the Friday service is the only religious practice he follows regularly. Life is quite different in western Java, where people follow Moslem practices very strictly. Yet even here the practices are blended in with age-old Indonesian beliefs and traditions.

Abdullah,* age 15, is the son of a rice farmer. He goes to high school but he also helps with work on the farm. His working day begins at dawn — and so does his religious day. Like Moslems in the Middle East, Abdullah prays five times a day, the first time at dawn and the last time at sunset. Wherever he is, he kneels down on the ground facing west. He thus looks toward the holy city of Mecca.

After the morning prayer, Abdullah goes out to work with his father in the rice field. They cut the rice plants carefully, in a special way, so that they will not disturb Deva Sri,* the rice goddess. This practice is part of an ancient belief in spirits which is practiced in Indonesia but not in other parts of the Moslem world (see Chapter 14). Most Indonesian rice farmers, whatever religion they follow, show the same respect for Deva Sri.

Like Nawi, Abdullah goes to his mosque at noon on Fridays. The mosque in Abdullah's village is an old building, richly decorated. A Moslem rule discourages painting or sculpture of any animal or human forms. But no such ban exists in the older religions of Southeast Asia. So some Indonesians have compromised. In Abdullah's mosque there are designs which look like leaves and flowers when seen close up. But at a distance these designs merge into pictures of human faces and figures.

Moslems have their own calendar for religious occasions. Abdullah knows that next week the holy month of Ramadan* begins. In Indonesia, this month is known as puasa,* which means "a fast." During the 30 days of Ramadan, Moslems are not allowed to eat or drink anything between sunrise and sunset. Abdullah wonders if his mother will be well enough for the fasting, since she had a slight fever this morning. If she is still sick when Ramadan begins, she will be excused from fasting — but she will have to make up the time when she is well.

Abdullah's big dream is of one day traveling to Mecca. This is a pilgrimage which all Moslems are expected to make once in their lives, if they can. Abdullah has heard one of the elders of the mosque talk about his own pilgrimage to Mecca. It was the most wonderful experience of his life, the man said.

During the time of the pilgrimage, hundreds of thousands of Moslems crowd into Mecca from all parts of the world. Sooner or later, all of them make their way to the Kaaba,* the holy shrine of Islam. The Kaaba stands in the courtyard of the Great Mosque in the middle city. Pilgrims who go there circle the Kaaba seven times. They kiss the holy black stone in one wall of the Kaaba. It was here that Mohammed swept away the old Arab idols 13 centuries ago and proclaimed the Word of God.

Abdullah realizes that the odds are against the son of an Indonesian farmer ever making the pilgrimage to Mecca. His family does not earn much money. Mecca is more than 5,000 miles away, and travel is expensive. Few Indonesians can make the journey.

All the same, Abdullah is sure he will find a way. After all, he has a whole lifetime ahead of him.

Chapter 14

Faiths Far and Near

MEASURED BY THE NUMBERS OF FOLLOWERS they command, Buddhism and Islam are the two dominant religions of Southeast Asia. Yet they exist side by side with a mixture of other faiths. Some of these other faiths have grown up in Southeast Asia, and some have been imported. Let's take a closer look at six of them:

Animism. At its simplest, animism might be described as a sort of nature worship. In Southeast Asia it's the oldest religion of all. It developed separately on other continents and is still found in many parts of the world.

Animism is based on the idea that all things in nature are alive. Animists believe such things are guided, or *animated*, by spirits. Animists believe there are spirits living in the trees, the streams, the rocks, the wind, the sun, and so on. If an animist wants to chop down a tree, he must first pray or make an offering to the tree's spirit. If he wants the wind to bring rain for his crops, then he must ask for help from the wind's spirit.

Today Southeast Asia has few people who practice animism and nothing else. Those who do are found only in remote areas such as the hills of Laos or the jungles of Indonesia's Kalimantan. But animism has left its mark on other religions and on the daily lives of many people. As one Western-educated Indonesian says: "I can still name more than 80 kinds of spirits and more than 50 devils." And a Malaysian newspaper recently ran a story with this headline: "Spirit in Tree Served Notice to Quit."

Hinduism. This religious faith had its origins in India. It was the first foreign religion to sweep into Southeast Asia. Around the first century A.D., Indians began to move eastward. They brought their religion with them, and it finally spread as far as the southern Philippines and central Vietnam.

Hindus believe that the universe is a wonderful structure in which everything and everybody fits into its proper place. One result is that Indians were divided into social classes known as castes, and no one could move outside the class he or she was born into. But Hindus also believe that people are reborn — and the next time around they may take a step up. In the end, if they lead good lives, they will leave this world and join the supreme spirit of the universe.

Since people on earth cannot know what this supreme spirit is, Hindus do not worship it directly. Instead, they worship many gods, each of which represents some different power of the supreme spirit. Hindus are free to choose just which of these gods they will worship.

In most of Southeast Asia, Hinduism never really took root. Buddhism replaced it in most mainland countries (see Chapter 12). But Hinduism has held out on the Indonesian island of Bali. Bali is a kind of "Little India" in the middle of a Moslem nation.

The Hinduism of Bali has changed quite a lot from the Hinduism of India. Unlike Indian Hindus, for example, the Balinese do not consider the cow a sacred animal. Also, their caste system never became as rigid as in India, where people in each caste were limited to certain kinds of jobs. In Bali, people were always allowed to take any job they could get.

Christianity. This was the last major religion to reach Southeast Asia. Europeans started to introduce it to the region about the 15th century A.D. When Spain took the Philippines, it built churches and sent missionaries to staff them. The missionaries spread Roman Catholicism as far as they could.

Today the Philippine Republic is the only Southeast Asian country with a majority of Christians. They make up more than 90 percent of the population. Of these, more than 80 percent are Roman Catholics.

The Filipinos have added their own colorful touches to Christian celebrations. Processions and ceremonies take place on saints' days and other festivals throughout the year. Each village chooses a saint to protect it, and on that saint's day the villagers hold a big festival. There is a procession to and from the village church, and then everyone cuts loose at a kind of fair, with feasting, games, and fireworks.

Outside the Philippines, Christianity made its greatest impact in Vietnam. There it was first introduced by French missionaries and settlers. Today about two-and-a-half million Vietnamese are Roman Catholics.

On the Indonesian island of Bali, rice is a main source of life. To protect the crop, the Balinese observe an animist ritual by making offerings to the rice gods. This woman is neatly spreading out her offering of rice cakes, fruits, and flowers.

Vietnam gives the clearest example of the kind of mixing of religions that has taken place throughout the countries of Southeast Asia. Most Vietnamese are Buddhists — but with some extra touches. Nearly all of them have a shrine at home where they worship the spirits of their dead ancestors. Some will consult an astrologer or fortune-teller about the best time for holding a marriage, planting their crops, or arranging some other important event.

These "extra touches" come from China, Vietnam's giant neighbor to the north. The Chinese spread many of their ideas into Vietnam, including those of two religions: Confucianism and Taoism.*

Confucianism. This set of teachings stemmed from the thoughts of a Chinese sage named Confucius, who lived in the sixth century B.C. Confucius did not claim to be a religious leader. But he did have many ideas about the best way to lead a good life.

One key idea was that people should trust one another. Ordinary people should obey their rulers, and the rulers should help the ordinary people. As Confucius saw it, this system began in the family, where the older people were the "rulers." Confucius also believed that when the older people died their souls stayed on with the family. All of this led to keeping a family shrine and worshiping one's ancestors.

Taoism. This faith started out in China as a belief that people should try to be satisfied with their lives. In the Chinese language, the word "tao" means "the way" — as in "that's the way things are" or "that's the way it goes." Taoists believe you can't change the way things are going to happen. Since you can't change things, they figure there's no point in worrying about it or struggling against it.

Mourners march through a Vietnamese town in a funeral parade for a Cao Dai leader.

176

Still, there's nothing in Taoism which says you can't try to find out the way things are going to happen. By making the effort, Taoists believe you can steer clear of the worst. So over the centuries more and more Taoists took up astrology, fortune-telling, and other methods of peeking into the future. This is the kind of Taoism that's found mixed in with other beliefs in Vietnam today.

Cao Dai.* With all these religions running into each other in Vietnam, the next step was for someone to bring them all together in one big new religion. That's just what some Vietnamese did back in 1926. They declared that the leaders of the world's major religions — including Jesus Christ, Buddha, and Confucius — were all forms of One God. They named this God — and their religion — Cao Dai.

To give an idea of just how wide-ranging Cao Dai is, its roster of saints includes Benjamin Franklin, Joan of Arc, Queen Elizabeth I of England, former Chinese president Sun Yat-sen,* and French poet Victor Hugo. In the 1950's, when Cao Dai was at its peak, it had more than two million followers. Today it has lost much of its influence.

Old and new, big and small, homegrown and imported, the variety of religions in Southeast Asia may look bewildering from a distance. But the people on the spot see things differently.

They may not believe that all religions can be fitted into one, like the followers of Cao Dai. But for thousands of years they have lived on a crossroads of different ideas. To them, there is nothing at all strange about the rich pattern of beliefs that runs through their daily lives.

Filipino women, carrying candles and wearing Spanish-style scarves called mantillas, enter a Roman Catholic church.

Double-check

Review

1. Gautama taught his followers what Four Truths?

2. Why do Buddhists think it's wrong to kill any creature, even a tiny insect?

3. Why do Abdullah and his father cut their rice plants carefully, in a special way?

4. What pilgrimage are all Moslems expected to make once in their lives, if they can?

5. What was the first foreign religion to sweep into Southeast Asia?

Discussion

1. Southeast Asia is known for its religious tolerance. Does religious tolerance make people *more* or *less* religious? Do you think religion is as important in the lives of most Americans as it is in the lives of most Southeast Asians? Why, or why not?

2. The roles of women were different in the Arab society of Mohammed's time and in Indonesia when Islam arrived there. Are there specific roles that you think women *should* fill in a society? Are there specific roles that men *should* fill in a society? Give reasons for your answers. How have women's roles and men's roles changed in the last century? Why do you think these changes have occurred?

3. What effect does the caste system have on people? Do you think most Hindus probably feel comfortable with it? Why, or why not? How would people in the U.S. feel if they were subject to a caste system?

Activities

1. Some students might research and report on the life and teachings of Buddha and the spread of Buddhist philosophy throughout Southeast Asia.

2. A Moslem or an Islamic scholar might be invited to speak to the class. Some students might look at the Koran before the visit and prepare a list of questions about its philosophy.

3. A committee of students might pretend to create a new religion that would be for everyone, as the Vietnamese did in 1926. What would it include? Why?

Skills

*Ignoble men, after obtaining favors,
revert to their natural disposition.
A dog's tail, after every possible
annointing and bending, returns
to its natural twist.*

— A Hindu Proverb

Use the passage above and information in Chapters 12, 13, and 14 to answer the following questions.

1. What is the subject of this proverb?
(a) dogs' tails (b) human nature (c) ignoble men

2. This passage is probably *not* which of the following?
(a) one of Gautama's Four Truths
(b) a teaching of Mohammed
(c) either of these

3. People in which of the following countries would be most likely to know this proverb?
(a) Bali (b) Burma (c) Indonesia

4. Which of these statements best sums up the proverb?
(a) Men get favors.
(b) Humans are ignoble.
(c) You can't change human nature.
(d) Humans are reborn as dogs.

Chapter 15

Words, Music, Action

SINCE IT IS SATURDAY, Beth Villahermosa (see page 88) has slept late. When she finally leaves her bedroom, a serving woman is walking by.

"*Magandang umaga,*"* says the servant.

"*Magandang umaga,*" says Beth.

She walks into the dining room.

"*Buenos días, Papá,*" she says.

Her father, a lawyer, is seated at the table drinking coffee with a neighbor, another lawyer.

Beth nods to the neighbor. "Good morning," she says. "Please excuse me."

With her father, Beth spoke Spanish. This was the official language during the 400 years that the Philippines belonged to Spain.

With the neighbor, Beth spoke English, the medium of instruction in schools and universities. English has been used there since the Philippines became a U.S. territory in 1898. In fact, so many people in the Philippines speak English, that the island nation has been called the third biggest English-speaking country in the world—after the U.S. and Britain.

All three languages are taught in Philippine schools. The government hopes that Pilipino will one day become the "home" language of everyone in the country. But there's some way to go. Right now, about 90 different local languages are spoken in the Philippines — and five or six of these are spoken by more than two million people *each*.

Indonesia faces the same problem, only worse. More than 100 different languages are spoken on Indonesia's many islands. When the country became independent in 1949, its new leaders launched a drive for one national language. They chose as a base an up-to-date version of popular or market Malay, the chief language of the Malay Peninsula. It was spoken also by many Indonesians along the coasts of the larger islands. Then they mixed in many technical words from Dutch, English, French, and German. They called their new language Bahasa* Indonesia, or just plain Indonesian. Nowadays it is widely spoken throughout the country.

The local languages spoken in Indonesia, the Philippines, and Malaysia belong to the same family. This doesn't mean that the different peoples can understand each other when they speak in their own tongues. But many words are the same, or almost the same, in more than one language. When Indonesians

183

❧ Southeast Asian music has a heavy beat, a lot of minor beats, and a melody floating across the top of it all.

and Malaysians talk about their freedom from colonial rule, for example, they both call it *merdeka*.*

North of Malaysia, this "family likeness" stops. The languages of the Southeast Asian mainland aren't very much like one another. Most of them are written very differently too.

Burmese, Thai, and Cambodian each have their own written alphabets. On the other hand, Vietnamese uses the Roman alphabet, which was brought in by European missionaries some 300 years ago. But don't think that makes it easy. Vietnamese has so many different accent marks that there are 18 ways of writing just the letter "A."

Even so, travelers through mainland Southeast Asia notice one thing that several of the languages have in common. It has been said that many people of this area don't talk, they sing. The reason is that the Thai, Lao, Vietnamese, and Burmese languages depend on tones. A word spoken with a high tone may mean something entirely different from the "same" word spoken with a low tone. And one language — Thai — has as many as five tones.

The idea of getting your meaning across by "singing" may seem strange — but there's something a bit like it in English. For example, if you say "Great!" you can mean two opposite things. If you say it with a high or rising tone, you mean "very good." But if you say it with a low or falling tone, you mean "that's bad" — you're annoyed.

One keynote of Southeast Asian music is its use of percussion instruments. This Javanese musician is doing his turn on a xylophone.

☆ ☆ ☆ ☆ ☆ ☆ ☆ ☆ ☆

In a part of the world where speech can be musical, it's not surprising that music itself is popular. In much of Indonesia, for example, every village has its own traditional orchestra, known as a *gamelan.* * It has been estimated that the total number of gamelans in Indonesia runs to 27,000 — which adds up to a lot of music.

Of course, in the cities of Southeast Asia young people may listen to Western rock more than the traditional music. Still, the influence hasn't all been one way. Long ago, the Laotians invented a musical instrument made of small tubes of bamboo tied together. European travelers heard it, liked it — and brought home the idea for the harmonica.

Although each country has its own style of music, all make use of similar instruments. The Indonesian gamelan includes a kind of flute, a kind of cello, and a lot of percussion instruments — xylophone, gongs, and drums. The biggest drum is known as a *kendang* * (which gives an idea of the way it sounds). The traditional Burmese orchestra contains instruments such as flutes and oboes — along with a xylophone, gongs, and drums. And orchestras in Laos and Cambodia also have their share of xylophones, gongs, and drums.

The result is a kind of basic Southeast Asian "sound." It has a heavy beat, a lot of minor beats around it, and a melody floating across the top of it all.

Southeast Asians probably got their "sound" from listening to Chinese and Indian music hundreds of years ago. Chinese and Indian influences can be found not only in music but in all the arts of Southeast Asia. But Southeast Asians haven't just copied their two big neighbors. They have often taken Chinese and Indian styles and turned them into something uniquely their own.

Take the field of architecture, for example. Many of the ancient ruins of Angkor in Cambodia were originally built as Hindu temples, at the time when Hinduism was *the* religion of Southeast Asia (*see* Chapter 14). Just the sheer size of these temples is impressive. Angkor Wat covers just under one square mile, or nearly 20 times the area of the Pentagon in Washington, D.C.

But Angkor is magnificent to look at not only from a distance but also from close up, in its smallest details. Its stone surfaces are carved with thousands of pictures showing ancient Cambodian history and legends. You can walk for hours on end past row after row of gods, kings, soldiers, dancers, and elephants — one of the grandest art shows ever designed.

Southeast Asians don't build Hindu temples today. But in their other arts they still show the same delight in thinking big and small at the same time. A case in point is to be found in Burma. During big festivals, the Burmese enjoy a show called a *pwe,** a mixture of theater, dancing, music, and comedy numbers. It's usually put on in the open air, and people sit on mats to watch and listen.

The show begins with traditional music. Then there are some dancing and comedy numbers. Finally, there's a classical play full of mythical characters — princes, wizards, spirits, talking animals, and so on. But the play is always updated with incidents and jokes about things that are happening in the world today.

The pwe may sound a bit like a TV variety show. But there's at least one big difference — it usually lasts all night, perhaps from nine P.M. to six A.M.

And this kind of marathon mixture of the arts is found in many parts of Southeast Asia — especially out in the villages.

On Java, the most populous island of Indonesia, a favorite entertainment is a kind of puppet show in which the shadows of the puppets are thrown onto a screen. There's a gamelan to play along with the show and provide music between the acts. And the whole show, like the pwe, can go on all night.

In the cities, of course, Southeast Asians can and do go to the movies. Some even have TV. But to the average Southeast Asian, even a three-hour movie may seem brief compared to the traditional shows.

The arts are a part of daily life in Southeast Asia. There are no neat dividing lines showing just where work or sports or religion ends and the arts begin. A Vietnamese may look like an artist as he paints designs on a bowl with great delicacy and skill. But as far as he's concerned, he's simply earning a living. A teenage girl in a Philippine village may be as skillful in her dancing as a Western ballerina. But for her, this skill is part of her religious life, since she dances only at the big Roman Catholic festivals.

One evening a Burmese orchestra plays music for a pwe. A few days later, the same orchestra provides music for — a boxing match. Don't be surprised! Boxing in Burma, and in other nearby countries, is partly a kind of dance.

Still, Burmese boxing is also a fast and bruising kind of sport. So even though there's no real dividing line between sports and the arts, it's simpler to draw one — and deal with dancing boxers in the next chapter.

Chapter 16

A Sense of Balance

"WHAT SPORTS are popular in your country?"

"Football, swimming, cycling, basketball, boxing...."

No, it isn't an American who's answering the question, but a Thai. All these sports *are* popular in Thailand — at least in the cities and towns. The story is much the same in other parts of Southeast Asia too.

So far, Southeast Asians have not won any international contests in sports such as soccer or basketball. One reason may have something to do with size. In soccer, a lightweight player is at a disadvantage when confronting a heavier opponent. In basketball, it helps to be tall. And compared to many peoples, Southeast Asians are short and light.

But when it comes to sports where size makes no difference, Southeast Asians are often right up there on top. Back in the 1800's, an English duke invented the game of badminton. In recent years, several of the

The Thais go in for fierce boxing matches in which a boxer can punch, kick, wrestle, or trip his opponent.

world's champion badminton players have come from Indonesia.

Southeast Asians enjoy games which involve skill, gracefulness, and speed. Not surprisingly, the games they invented for themselves require a lot of all three. Take the kind of "football" that's played, with variations, in many parts of the region. In the Philippines it's known as *sipa*.* In Malaysia it has the grander name of *Sepak Raga Jaring*.* For the Thais, it's *takraw*.* In Burma, it's known as *chinlon*.*

In the old days chinlon was a game for boys only, but today girls are encouraged to play it too. The ball is about four inches in diameter. It's made of bamboo strips and there are holes in its surface, so it's light.

The players stand in a fairly large circle. One player throws the ball up and then kicks it up in the air. From that point on, the idea is to see how long the players can keep the ball off the ground, touching it only with their legs.

They can kick the ball using their knees, even let it fall behind them and flick it up with their heels. There's a whole range of "strokes," from the simple to the tricky, and a good chinlon player can keep up a solo performance that's as dazzling as a juggling act. A player can keep the ball for as long as he or she wants, so long as the ball never touches the ground. The point is that the players are playing *with*, not *against*, one another.

They are not trying to make other players drop the ball. They're working together, like a single volleyball team. And when Burmese people go to a chinlon game played by experts, they're watching an exhibition, not a contest.

Other sports of the area are also more or less for

Compare this photo of a Thai boxing match with matches in the U.S. How do the two seem to differ?

"show." An example is the Indonesian self-defense known as *penchak*.* Penchak is a kind of boxing, often accompanied by music as if it were a dance. But in some parts of Indonesia, the penchak is much more like dancing than fighting, and the "boxers" rarely hit each other at all.

Of course, Southeast Asians do have their competitive sports, and some of them are quite rough. The Burmese and Thais, for example, go in for fierce boxing matches in which a boxer can punch, kick, wrestle, or trip his opponent, even jab him with his elbow or butt him with his head. In fact the boxers can do almost anything but bite, claw, or pull hair.

All of this takes place at a tremendous pace — a straight left foot to the jaw followed at once by a right elbow to the stomach. Yet the boxers are so skilled at dodging and countering that they rarely get seriously hurt. If a boxer is in trouble, his opponent will at once hold off. The crowd doesn't come to see bloodshed, but a display of skill.

One of the most competitive sports of the area is a game which Westerners use to relax. It's a common game in Bangkok, the capital city of Thailand, where Anek lives. When he wants to see a real knock-down, drag-out contest, he goes to watch — kite-flying.

Kite-flying contests are held in Bangkok every Sunday in the spring, when the monsoon winds are blowing strong. Thailand's best kite men meet in a public park near the royal palace, and thousands of fans turn up — along with Anek — to watch them.

Each contest involves a duel between two different types of kites. One type of kite is called a *chula*,* which is 12 feet long. This huge kite acts as the attacker in the contest. In a high wind, the chula's pull is so strong that three or four men have to hold on to the string.

The chula chases a much smaller kite called an *epow.** This is only about two feet long. The chula tries to capture the epow by tangling with its string. But that isn't so easy. The small epow is much faster than the heavy chula. In fact, the epow often wins the contest by making the chula chase it down too close to the ground, so that the chula loses the wind and crashes.

Southeast Asians enjoy a slam-bang contest — especially when a gamble is involved. In Thailand many people bet on bull races. In Malaysia, Indonesia, and the Philippines, they bet on cock fights — battles to the death between specially trained roosters. In Singapore people bet on the Chinese game *Mah Jongg** — a complicated game of dominoes played with dice and 136 pieces known as tiles.

Perhaps the Southeast Asians' love of sports has something to do with their history. Over the centuries, these people have worked very hard to survive. And their favorite sports may suggest how they did it — by using much the same skill and grace it takes to keep a kite, a chinlon ball, or a boxer from crashing to the ground.

Double-check

Review

1. About how many different local languages are spoken in the Philippines?

2. Why has it been said that many people of Southeast Asia don't talk, they sing?

3. What two major influences can be found in all the arts of Southeast Asia?

4. In Burma, what is football known as?

5. What is *Mah Jongg?*

Discussion

1. The people in several Southeast Asian countries speak *many* different languages. What are some advantages and disadvantages of such linguistic diversity within a country? How would it affect schooling? Road signs? Shopping? Newspapers? Should each country adopt *one* official language? Why, or why not? If so, how?

2. Western rock music has been popular in large cities throughout Southeast Asia. Why do you think this has happened? Explain your answer.

3. What kinds of qualities and values are important in Southeast Asian sports? How are these similar to, or different from, the values of American sports? What, if anything, might this suggest about differences in the cultures of the two regions?

Activities

1. Several students might research and report on several different written alphabets used in Southeast Asia. Students might prepare a bulletin board display comparing the Roman alphabet letters with different Southeast Asian alphabets. If possible, a person familiar with one or more Southeast Asian languages might be invited to speak to the class, especially to illustrate the use of tones in the spoken languages of the region.

2. If possible, the class might listen to one or more recordings of various types of Southeast Asian music and then discuss their reactions to it.

3. Some students might select a Southeast Asian sport or art to research and then demonstrate it to the rest of the class.

Skills

LITERACY RATES* IN SOUTHEAST ASIA

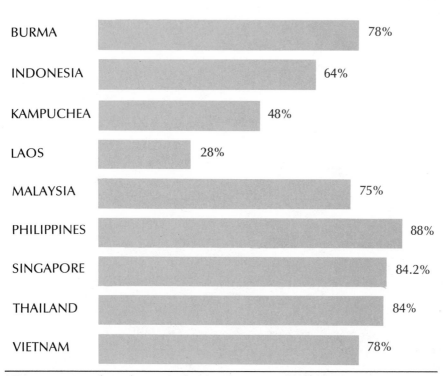

BURMA	78%
INDONESIA	64%
KAMPUCHEA	48%
LAOS	28%
MALAYSIA	75%
PHILIPPINES	88%
SINGAPORE	84.2%
THAILAND	84%
VIETNAM	78%

*Citizens age 15 and up who can read and write   Source: *The 1985 CIA World Factbook*

Use the bar graph above and information in Chapters 15 and 16 to answer the following questions.

1. What does this graph show? Which country is missing?

2. In which country is the literacy rate the highest? In which is it the lowest?

3. In how many countries are more than 25% of the people illiterate?

4. What percentage of citizens in which country do not know 18 ways of writing the letter "A"?

5. What order are the countries on the graph arranged in? For the purposes of a bar graph, what other order of arrangement might have been better? Why?

195

5

LIFE IN A LAND AT WAR

Chapter 17

The Agony of Indochina

TIME HAS PLAYED its role, and the images have faded from most minds. But once they were fresh and heartbreaking, glaring at us every night from the TV set. There were refugees, desperate to flee from the fighting. There were the dead, the dying, and the injured, often innocent bystanders who happened to be in the wrong place at the wrong time. There were the orphans, children caught up in a war they did not understand.

Images like these helped make the Indochina war the most unpopular the U.S. ever fought. It deeply divided the American people. It became a prime political issue. In 10 years of war, the U.S. lost more than 45,000 troops killed in action and more than 10,000 missing.

Each of these figures was a separate tragedy of its own. But in numbers, the totals were small compared to casualties among the people of Indochina. In South Vietnam alone, more than 150,000 government troops were reported killed, and civilian casualties

In the 1960's the U.S. press carried many photos such as this one. It shows U.S. troops moving the body of a dead soldier through a Vietnamese clearing. How do you suppose such photos might have affected American reactions to the war?

were estimated at 425,000. No accurate count was available for North Vietnamese casualties, but some experts estimated a total of 900,000.

And all this had occurred within 20 years of the Geneva Agreements of 1954, which at the time were expected to solve Indochina's troubles (see page 153). How had it come to this?

The story of the U.S. military role in Indochina is complex and controversial. People naturally hold very strong views about the war, and there is not too much that all sides will agree on.

However, in describing those controversial years, we can identify 12 steps from the Geneva Agreements of 1954 to the Communist take-over of Indochina.

1. *Geneva Agreements break down.* Within months of the agreements, Ngo Dinh Diem,* the South Vietnamese president, refuses to hold elections. He says free elections are impossible in the north, so he won't hold them in the south.

2. *Fighting breaks out again.* After the breakdown of the Geneva Agreements, fighting resumes. Between 1954 and 1962, there is a steady increase in guerrilla activity by South Vietnamese Communists known as the Viet Cong,* who are aided by North Vietnam. In 1955 the U.S. helps to train members of the South Vietnamese army. By 1960 U.S. advisers in South Vietnam number 685, and weapons and supplies are flowing to the South Vietnamese army.

3. *The U.S. is drawn in.* Even with U.S. aid and advisers, the situation fails to improve. With the help of North Vietnam, the Viet Cong makes wide gains throughout South Vietnam. U.S. troops begin entering the country. In November 1963, a faction of the South Vietnamese army stages a coup. Diem is ousted from office and murdered. A series of coups follows. The military situation continues to get worse.

4. *The U.S. begins bombing the North.* Alleged attacks on two U.S. destroyers in the Gulf of Tonkin by North Vietnam prompts U.S. President Lyndon Johnson to order air attacks against bases in the North in 1964. Johnson gets the "Gulf of Tonkin" resolution from Congress. It gives him a free hand "to take all necessary steps, including the use of armed force," to protect U.S. interests.

No one can bring back the lives that have been lost. But something can be done to repair the shattered land.

5. *The war at its height.* Beginning in 1965, the U.S. involvement increases dramatically. U.S. planes bomb North Vietnam frequently. U.S. troops increase. In the U.S., escalation is supported by many, but there is also widespread opposition. There are protests and demonstrations across the U.S. The war continues to escalate. By early 1968, the U.S. has half a million men in South Vietnam.

6. *Tet offensive.* U.S. officials report that the Communists are weakening. However, on January 30, 1968, the start of the Buddhist holiday called *Tet,* the Communists launch a massive offensive all over South Vietnam. The attack is eventually beaten back, but not before tremendous casualties on both sides and among civilians.

7. *Peace talks begin.* In a dramatic television speech, President Johnson says he will not run for reelection in 1968. He halts the bombing of most of North Vietnam and asks for peace talks. Opposing sides agree, and talks begin in May 1968 in Paris, France. Progress is slow.

8. *U.S. role widens in Laos and Cambodia.* Fighting between pro- and anti-Communist forces plus the use of two countries by North Vietnam to supply its forces in the South prompts the U.S. to begin secret bombing operations in Laos and Cambodia. In May 1970 the U.S. and South Vietnam openly send combat forces into Cambodia. Forces soon withdraw.

Solemn and silent, a Vietnamese boy surveys the ruins of a community smashed by war.

9. *Vietnamization.* President Richard Nixon puts forward a policy of "Vietnamization" of the war. This means having the South Vietnamese take over more and more of the fighting from Americans. U.S. troop reductions accelerate. But the U.S. role in the air war is stepped up as bombing increases.

10. *End of U.S. involvement.* Secret peace talks are held between the U.S. and the North Vietnamese. U.S. troop strength continues to drop. By autumn 1972 there are no U.S. ground-combat troops fighting in Vietnam. But bombing continues. On January 27, 1973 a cease-fire is signed in Paris officially ending the Vietnam war. But heavy fighting continues in some areas of Vietnam, even though the U.S. has no active role in it. In August 1973, U.S. bombing in Cambodia ends, marking the close of U.S. combat operations in Indochina.

11. *South Vietnam falls.* Despite the end of U.S. participation, fighting continues throughout Indochina and Communists make steady gains in Cambodia, Laos, and South Vietnam. In early 1975, the South Vietnamese army retreats to the highly populated lowlands, triggering a massive panic. The South Vietnamese army collapses and thousands of refugees flee the country. In April 1975 the Communists take over South Vietnam. In 1976 the country is officially reunited. In 1978 it joins the Soviet trade bloc.

12. *Indochina under Communist rule.* Communists also make steady gains in Cambodia and Laos. Cambodia falls to Communists just days before South Vietnam collapses. Within a matter of months, Laotian Communists have taken control in that country. The new government calls Cambodia "Kampuchea." They cut the country off from all contact with the rest of the world. Millions of people perish; thousands of others flee as refugees.

Double-check

Review

1. What was the most unpopular war the U.S. ever fought?

2. What were the South Vietnamese Communists known as?

3. What did the Gulf of Tonkin resolution give President Johnson?

4. What did "Vietnamization" mean?

5. What was signed in Paris in January 1973?

Discussion

1. The Vietnam war was called "the war fought on TV." What does this mean? How might the intensive media coverage have affected U.S. citizens' reactions to the war? Should governments permit such extensive media coverage of their wars? Why, or why not?

2. Which of the 12 steps outlined in this chapter do you think was the most important step in escalating the war? Why? Which was the most important step in ending the war? Why?

3. What role, if any, should the U.S. government take in the rebuilding of Vietnam and other war-ravaged countries? Give reasons for your answer.

Activities

1. If possible, a Vietnam veteran might be invited to speak to the class about his experiences in the war and his experiences upon returning home.

2. Some students might role-play a conversation, about the war, between President Johnson, President Nixon, and the Vietnamese boy pictured in this chapter.

3. Some students might research and report on the current military situations in Vietnam, Cambodia, and Laos.

Skills

A PARTIAL CHRONOLOGY OF THE INDOCHINA WAR

1954

1955   A. Gulf of Tonkin resolution passes.

1963   B. U.S. trains the South Vietnamese army.

        C. U.S. forces openly enter Cambodia.

1964

        D. Peace talks begin in Paris.

1968

        E. Geneva Agreements begin to break down.

1968   F. Cease-fire agreement signed in Paris.

1970   G. South Vietnam falls.

        H. U.S. pulls ground forces out of Vietnam.

1972

        I. Communists launch Tet offensive.

1973

        J. Diem is murdered.

1975

Use the events listed above and information in Chapter 17 to do the following on a separate sheet of paper. Write the years down the left side of the paper. Then write the letter of each event next to the year in which it happened. (The events are not in the correct order in the list above.)

Chapter 18

Vietnam: The Scars Remain

BIRDS HAVE RETURNED to the little villages near the city of Can Tho* in southern Vietnam. Larks sing in the tall grasses, and sparrows chirp once more in the banyan trees. No longer is their music interrupted by the dreaded thud of mortars. Peace has come to some villages of the Mekong River delta, which have known so little peace.

To all outward appearances, life in these hamlets goes on as usual. The rivers of the delta still roll on through the flat countryside as timelessly as the tides. Dragonflies still buzz menacingly in the clearings, and water buffalo still slog through the fields. Here and there farmers in their pajamalike work clothes and cone-shaped hats tend their crops as they have done for centuries. Now it all seems as it must once have seemed so long ago — before the war.

But beneath the surface of life in the delta are the scars left by more than a quarter-century of conflict. This conflict has altered lives beyond reckoning and brought suffering to millions. No one knows the re-

A Vietnamese boy searches for his father's
body, believed to have been buried in a mass grave.

sults of the conflict better than 15-year-old Tran
Dinh Vien.* For the war has robbed him of his family
and left him almost completely on his own.

Vien (he goes by his given name, which comes last
in his country) once knew the closeness of Vietnamese family life. When he was younger, he lived
with his father, mother, and sister in a thatched cottage by the side of an irrigation canal. Next door lived
Vien's uncle, his wife and children, and Vien's grandmother. All the adult members of the family spent
their days working side by side in the fields.

Like most Vietnamese farmers, Vien's father put
his family ahead of everything else, even himself.
From the time of his son's birth, Mr. Tran tried to set
a proper example for the boy by the life he led. He
gave the boy no speeches, and he never made com-

✍ For many Vietnamese, not being able to bury one's ancestors is a sign of very bad luck.

mands. Nonetheless, Vien learned to follow the older man's wishes without a second thought.

Vien was proudest of his father on those special days when the family paid a visit to the ancestors' tombs. As the family's oldest living male, Vien's father would be the leader of these outings. When the special day came, the family members would dress in their finest clothes. Vien's father would hail a water taxi from the banks of the canal. Then the entire family would climb aboard the motorboat and ride about a mile downstream.

At the tombs, Mr. Tran would conduct a simple ceremony in honor of the spirits of the ancestors. The family would light small sticks of incense which stood before the family memorial. They would then say prayers to all the ancestors and sometimes offer them gifts. Once the ceremony was over, Mr. Tran would hail another water taxi, and all would return home.

Vien has often heard his grandmother speak longingly of those days. "Belief in our ancestors was stronger then," she maintains. "We never had any fear of soldiers or guns or people who would harm us. We looked to our families for protection, and somehow we got along."

Things changed when Vien was seven. At about that time, his father was drafted into the South Vietnamese army and was sent to fight in a distant city. Vien's uncle became the head of Vien's family, and his grandmother moved into Vien's cottage to keep his mother company. At about this same time, Vien began to go to a Buddhist school.

One afternoon, while Vien was at school, his mother and sister boarded a water taxi to go to market in Can Tho. That was the last the family saw of them, for they never returned home. Vien's uncle guesses that their water taxi became the target of a Viet Cong ambush. No one knows exactly what happened because no bodies were ever recovered.

For many Vietnamese, not being able to bury one's ancestors is considered a sign of very bad luck. And sure enough, more bad luck did follow. When Vien's father received word of his wife's disappearance, he started immediately for home. On the way, however, he was shot by a Viet Cong sniper and killed. A farmer found his body and sent it home for burial.

All of these sudden deaths left Vien numb with disbelief. He went through the funeral ceremonies not knowing what to think. He stood by silently while family members dressed the body in the newest suit of clothes. He looked on absently while they covered his father's face with a white scarf — the symbol of the barrier between the living and the dead.

When all was in readiness, villagers came to the house to pay their last respects. Then the body was placed in a wooden coffin and taken downstream to the family tombs. Vien's grandmother placed a bowl of uncooked rice on the coffin to keep the body from rising from the dead. Then the coffin was placed in one of the tombs.

Vien did not realize his own sense of loss for many months thereafter. It dawned on him gradually as he paid more and more visits to his father's tomb. In time he came to understand his own role in the family scheme of things. As one of two surviving members of his immediate family, he was a main link between the ancestors and those still unborn.

Vien has lived on with his grandmother in the

thatched cottage by the side of the canal. He is determined to respect his father's spirit in every way he can. Now he works side by side with his uncle in the fields, just as his father once did. He even helps pay rent on the land to the landlord in Can Tho.

Vien feels closer to his uncle's family now than he ever did before. This closeness is most apparent during the Vietnamese New Year, Tet. Tet comes in the middle of the rainy season, usually in late January or early February by the Western calendar. The date changes from year to year because Tet is fixed according to the lunar calendar. That is, it takes place when the moon is in a certain phase.

For the Vietnamese, Tet is Christmas, New Year's, and the Fourth of July all rolled into one. Vien's relatives start getting ready for the celebration months in advance. Vien's aunt consults a fortune-teller to make sure the New Year will bring good luck. Vien's uncle invites the spirits of the ancestors to return to life and join the family celebration. Then, at the stroke of 12 on the scheduled day, the four-day holiday begins.

It usually starts off with the din of exploding firecrackers. The reason has to do with an old Vietnamese legend. This legend says that the evil spirits have a way of hanging about Vietnamese homes at the start of Tet. By keeping the noise up long enough, families hope to scare these spirits from their doors.

Vien enjoys spending Tet with his uncle and his family. He is fond of his younger cousins, and he always brings them several gifts. Even so, Vien wishes that his cousins would forget about the firecrackers. Legend or no legend, firecrackers remind Vien far too much of the guns of war.

☆　☆　☆　☆　☆　☆　☆　☆　☆

Ever since returning to the city of Hanoi, Le Truc

Mai* has felt a little sad. The hometown she has come back to is not the same as the one she left.

When Le Truc Mai rides the downtown trolley, she passes buildings shattered in U.S. air raids. When she bicycles to the airport, she sees craters left by bombs.

Le Truc Mai lives on a quiet city street. Her father is an official at Hanoi's Historical Museum. Among his duties, he keeps watch on a room dedicated to "The Heroic Struggle of the Vietnamese People Against Chinese Invaders." In the room are items from the thousand-year period, beginning in 111 B.C., when China ruled Vietnam as a colony.

Today bad feelings still exist between the two countries. In 1978 Vietnam began expelling its ethnic Chinese residents. More than 200,000 were forced to leave the country in small boats. Many of these "boat people" went to China, and some came to the U.S. But thousands of them perished at sea, and thousands still remain in Southeast Asian refugee camps.

In January 1979, Vietnam overthrew Cambodia's rulers and put in a new government. A month later, China invaded Vietnam. After a few battles, China withdrew, saying that it had wanted only to "teach Vietnam a lesson" about relations with its neighbors.

Mr. Le has long supported Vietnam against other countries. During the early 1950's, he joined a guerrilla movement, the Viet Minh,* formed to drive the French from Vietnam. Then the Le family lived in the city of Hue,* in the south. After the Geneva Agreements, the family moved to the Communist-run North.

So Le Truc Mai was born and raised in Hanoi, Vietnam's capital. When she first saw bombs falling on Hanoi, she was frightened by the smoke on the hori-

During the war, many Vietnamese spent a lot of time living underground.

zon and the blasts which shook the earth. Then, like her friends, she tried to resign herself to the bombing.

But as the air raids continued, Mr. Le grew concerned for his daughter's safety. One day he finally hit upon a plan to keep her safe. His cousin was a rice farmer in nearby Hung Yen* Province. Mr. Le would send his daughter to live with his cousin and go to a village school.

When he first told Le Truc Mai about the plan, she was upset. Although she never said so, she really didn't want to leave home. But then she realized that many of her friends in Hanoi were also leaving the city — and for the same reason. At least she would be lucky enough to live with relatives whom she knew.

And so she bid good-bye to her parents and boarded a bus for the fertile Red River country just east of Hanoi. At the other end of her trip, her father's cousins welcomed her as though she were their own daughter. Both of their sons were away, fighting in the North Vietnamese army. Thus, this couple was pleased to have a young person in their home again.

Le Truc Mai's school was a hut with walls of brick and a roof of palm thatch. From the time she began classes there, she liked the school and worked very hard to get good grades. Her teacher encouraged students to do their best by having them pretend that they were soldiers in the North Vietnamese army. The best student in class, the teacher said, would be the "first soldier" to enter the South Vietnamese capital of Saigon at the end of the war.

After school, Le Truc Mai helped out with the farm chores. Her father's cousins belonged to a farm cooperative — an organization in which farmers worked large plots of land as a group. Their cooperative had 400 members and was spread over several villages. Each worker had his or her job to do in the cooperative. In addition, each family had a small piece of land to cultivate on its own.

Le Truc Mai was given special charge of the family fish pond. Each afternoon she would spend 15 or 20 minutes feeding the carp which the family raised. Once or twice a week she would wade into the pond and pluck a carp from the water. Then she would take it home to her cousins' cottage to prepare for the evening meal.

Le Truc Mai lived with her cousins for about three years. At times, during lulls in the fighting, she would return to Hanoi on school vacation. But most of the time she stayed in Hung Yen Province. She rarely got homesick because she rarely had the time.

She missed her parents most during family religious services. Once every few weeks her cousins would gather at an altar in their cottage and burn incense sticks in memory of the dead. This way of noting the anniversary of an ancestor's death always made Le Truc Mai feel a little lonesome. It simply reminded her too much of home.

When the war finally ended, Le Truc Mai returned to Hanoi with some regret, for she had enjoyed her time in the countryside. Now she is unsure just where she will have to live in the years ahead. Her education has provided her with skills the government intends using. She will probably be sent to teach in some far-off part of the country, perhaps even in the remote highlands.

This prospect doesn't worry Le Truc Mai. In fact, she looks forward to it. Her years at Hung Yen changed her, she realizes, and she feels almost a country girl at heart. Besides, now that the war is over, Le Truc Mai realizes that a tremendous rebuilding job lies ahead, and she is eager to do her part in the effort.

Double-check

Review

1. What is a sign of very bad luck for many Vietnamese?

2. What is the Vietnamese New Year called?

3. Whom did Vietnam begin expelling in 1978?

4. What was the Viet Minh formed to do?

5. What is a farm cooperative?

Discussion

1. Vietnamese people give great honor to their ancestors. How does this affect their lives? How do people in the U.S. feel about their ancestors? How does this affect our lives? Give reasons to support your answers.

2. When the ethnic Chinese were forced out of Vietnam, several Southeast Asian countries were extremely reluctant to do anything to help them, and some governments even turned the boat people back out to sea rather than admit them as refugees. Why do you think this happened?

3. How long do you think it will take before northern and southern Vietnamese people forget the war and think of themselves as true equals in their country? How might their experience be similar to, or different from, what happened in the U.S. after the U.S. Civil War? Explain your answers.

Activities

1. Several students might role-play a conversation between Vien, Le Truc Mai, and other northern and southern Vietnamese young people. They could discuss the division of the country in the past and their thoughts about the future.

2. Some students might research and report on the resettlement of the boat people throughout the world. Others might report on the plight of other Southeast Asian refugees who were forced out of their homelands for a variety of reasons.

3. If possible, a Southeast Asian refugee might be invited to speak to the class about her or his experiences.

Skills

Seriously Ill

*My body has been battered under
the changing weather of China,
My heart is sorely troubled by
the misfortunes befallen Vietnam.
Oh, what a bitter thing it is
to fall ill in prison!
But, instead of weeping,
I prefer to keep singing.*

—From *The Prison Diary of Ho Chi Minh*

Use the passage above and information in Chapter 18 to answer the following questions.

1. This passage comes from which of the following?
(a) a song   (b) a diary   (c) a weather report

2. From which of these places was the author writing?
(a) prison   (b) his home   (c) a hospital

3. Ho favors which country?
(a) China   (b) Vietnam   (c) neither

4. Ho's mood in this poem could be described as which of the following?
(a) triumphant   (b) pessimistic   (c) optimistic

5. Ho's and many Vietnamese people's feelings about China may be traced to what event in history?
(a) China ruled Vietnam for 1,000 years.
(b) Vietnam ruled China for 1,000 years.
(c) Ho became ill in prison.

Chapter 19

Laos and Cambodia

RUNNING THROUGH the river valleys of northern Laos is a highway known as Route 13. It connects the Laotian capital of Vientiane with the city of Luang Prabang to the north. The highway serves as a commercial lifeline and is one of the region's busiest roads.

About halfway between these two Laotian cities, Route 13 slices through the little village of Muong Hom.* The village is not much more than a cluster of huts hugging the limestone hills above the road. Except for its one gasoline pump, Muong Hom has no landmarks to attract passing travelers. Its greatest attraction is Route 13 itself.

To one villager, 18-year-old Phoune Petrasy,* Route 13 has always held a special fascination. When he was much younger, Phoune would stand by the roadside for hours and wave at the passing cars and wagons. Back in those days Phoune thought it was exciting to have a highway running past his front yard.

Now he is not so sure, for the highway has also brought its share of trouble.

While Phoune was growing up, his village became a battleground for two competing armies. One was the government force. The other was the Communist-led force of the Pathet Lao.* Both sides sought to control Muong Hom in order to control traffic on Route 13. The struggle brought tragedy to many families of the village, including Phoune's.

Phoune lives with his mother and father and two younger sisters in one of Muong Hom's larger homes. Like the other houses of the village, Phoune's sits on stilts with a front porch at one end. Phoune's father is one of the wealthier rice farmers in the village. He grows much more rice than his family can eat.

Several years ago, Phoune's father was elected *pho ban** — head of the village government. He now must cooperate with the local People's Revolutionary Committee, which was set up in 1975, when the Pathet Lao took control of the country.

At the time of his election, Mr. Petrasy was in his early 50's. That made him unusually young to win such a job. But the civil war had taken the lives of some elders of the village, and it had frightened others. The villagers did not have an older man they could trust to lead them. So they turned to Mr. Petrasy because of his success as a farmer and his devotion to the Buddhist faith.

As headman, Mr. Petrasy has many duties. He must help settle disputes which arise between two or more village families. He must welcome strangers to the village. And he must keep villagers informed of what is happening within the national government in Vientiane and in the Revolutionary Committees.

To carry out his duties, Mr. Petrasy needs the respect of his townspeople. He has been an able head-

Young Laotian forces such as these fell to the Pathet Lao in 1975. Since then, thousands of Laotian refugees have fled to Thailand and other countries to escape Communist rule.

man because he has gotten the respect he needs. He would be fully satisfied with his life, were it not for one thing. His eldest son, Sisouk,* left home nine years ago and has never returned.

At the time of Sisouk's departure, the Pathet Lao had just taken control of Muong Hom from government forces. Laotian Communists were seeking young men to send to North Vietnam to be trained to fight in Laos. The Communists went to Mr. Petrasy and asked him to select some village recruits. Mr. Petrasy refused as graciously as possible. As village headman, he explained, he simply couldn't afford to take sides in the civil war.

At the same time Sisouk had reached his 13th birthday. At that point a Laotian boy is said to become a man, and villagers celebrate to mark the event. First Sisouk's hair was cut as a symbol of his manhood. Then the entire village turned out for a great feast.

Some of the local Pathet Lao rebels attended the feast. They sat and listened patiently while the village storyteller told of the founding of Muong Hom. At the end of the celebration, two soldiers approached Sisouk and told him they had selected him as a Pathet Lao trainee. They said that he would have to come with them, that he had no other choice.

So Sisouk left for North Vietnam that night. Phoune remembers his sorrow at having to say goodbye. Sisouk was gone for about three years before his family had any word of him. In the course of that time, Muong Hom was captured by government troops and then recaptured by the Pathet Lao.

Then one day, shortly after the Pathet Lao again took control of the village, news of Sisouk finally did arrive. A Communist soldier reported that Sisouk was not only alive but in the very next town.

Phoune was overjoyed. He hoped Sisouk would come home — and the sooner the better. But his mother and father did not share their son's enthusiasm. They had always tried to remain neutral as their village seesawed between one side and the other in the civil war. The idea of their son returning home from war wearing a Pathet Lao uniform disturbed them. They would have preferred that he stay away.

As it turned out, Sisouk never made the trip to Muong Hom. The military unit he was assigned to was shipped off to another town far to the south. When the Pathet Lao became the dominant force in Laos in 1975, Phoune's mother and father expected

Sisouk to come home. To their sadness, he never came.

The family has had word from him, however. A fellow soldier has reported that Sisouk has been sent south to Vientiane. His parents are glad that Sisouk is no longer on the battlefield. But now they worry about him in another way.

In most Laotian villages, young men become Buddhist novices when they reach the age of 20. At this time they enter a Buddhist monastery just as Maung Hla did in Burma at a younger age. The months in the monastery are thought to be very important ones for spiritual growth. Sisouk's parents fear that he may never enter a monastery at all.

For the moment, Phoune has nearly given up hope of ever seeing his only brother again. At times he feels quite bitter toward the Pathet Lao for taking Sisouk away. But his father has advised Phoune against such feelings. As Mr. Petrasy has told his son, bitterness will not bring Sisouk home.

In their discussions, Mr. Petrasy often cites an old Laotian proverb. It sums up the futility of taking sides. It goes: "The water drops, the ants eat the fish. The water rises, the fish eat the ants. So it is better to love than hate."

☆　☆　☆　☆　☆　☆　☆　☆　☆

In January 1975, Ang Eav* said farewell to her parents and brothers and boarded a train for Cambodia's capital city of Phnom Penh. It was the happiest day of her life, for the 16-year-old was going to the university to study to be a druggist. It was to be the first step in fulfilling an ambition she had had since she was a child.

Today, Ang Eav is a bitter refugee from Cambodia's Communist government. She is living in a small village in Thailand near the Cambodian border. With thousands of other Cambodian refugees, she is ill, living off charity, homesick, and with no chance of soon returning to her homeland. She has had no word of her parents since March 1975, and she doesn't know if they, or her brothers, are still alive.

Between her journey to Phnom Penh and her unhappy exile in Thailand lay seven frightening months of forced labor, disease, threats against her life, and near starvation. Like many other Cambodians, Ang Eav had little interest in politics. Yet like them she found herself a victim of Cambodia's bitter civil war.

Ang Eav had been in Phnom Penh only a few months when the Khmer Rouge,* Cambodia's Communist forces, took over the capital. On the day Phnom Penh fell, Ang went out into the streets to watch the conquerors enter the city. Excited by the scene but nervous about her future, she cheered and danced as the black-pajama-clad troops entered the city. She was amazed at the sight of the victors, for some of them, carrying submachine guns, grenade launchers, and mortars, seemed no older than 11 or 12.

Later that night, when the excitement had died down, an officer in a jeep pulled up at the university dormitories. Shouting into a bullhorn, he ordered all students out into the streets, and told them they were to march in formation to the outskirts of the city. On their march, the students could see that parts of the city were in flames. All over the city, people were on the march and the highways were jammed with Cambodians moving northward under the guard of Khmer Rouge soldiers.

Three miles outside of town, Ang and her fellow students were ordered to stop. All night, groups of weary Cambodians passed them, marching northward under the prod of the Khmer Rouge. It seemed to Ang that no one had been spared. Babies and children, the aged and the ill — even hospital patients — all were forced to march. She decided that the Khmer Rouge must have emptied Phnom Penh.

At dawn, the students were ordered to continue their march. No one told them where they were going. There was little water and little food, and the guards would not let them forage in the fields along the roads. For six days, the group marched northward, passing through towns and cities that were nearly all deserted. The corpses of the children, the aged, and the ill who had not been able to keep up lay on the road and in the gullies.

After six days, the students reached the town of Pursat, where they were ordered to stop. The area around the town was crowded with refugee families, so the students were marched to a remote rice paddy area. This was to be their new home.

Each day, the refugees were marched out to the fields to harvest the rice or build irrigation ditches. "A gong woke us each day at sunrise and we went to the fields where we worked until about noon, when we had an hour for lunch. Then we began again, and worked until it was dark. When we arrived home, the rice was already cooked — it was all we usually got, rice with some salt. Then on nights when there was a full moon, we went back to the fields and worked until about 11 o'clock."

At first the students believed they would go back to Phnom Penh after the rice was harvested. But one day, a Khmer Rouge officer told them that no one was to be allowed back into the capital city. Later, they heard that only Cambodians with industrial skills were being allowed to return to Phnom Penh.

Many of Ang's friends took sick and died at Pursat. There was little medicine available. What was available was dispensed by soldiers who could not read, and did not know what they were giving out. Ang knew the medicines, but she was not trusted. It was so crowded in the camp that Ang could get only two small cans of rice a day. There were no vegetables or meat.

One day in early 1976, they were marched to the railway station and put aboard empty boxcars. They were packed tightly into the cars — Ang says "like fish in a can." Then followed a bone-jarring eight-day trip toward the north. When they emerged from the train, they were in the northernmost section of Cambodia on the edge of a thick jungle. When Ang found that the town was only 30 miles from the Thai border, she resolved to escape.

Ang and a friend complained of sickness. The two were sent to the dispensary and treated for malaria. Security in the dispensary was lax, and one evening, Ang and her friend slipped away into the jungle. Eleven days later, bruised and bone tired, each with a genuine case of malaria, the two young people forded a river and were in Thailand.

"I have no news of my parents or my brothers," Ang says softly. "I suppose they are all planting rice somewhere. I don't know. Maybe they are dead." She would like to return to Cambodia, but knows she would be punished, perhaps killed. "This is no life," she says bitterly. "We did not support the old government," she says. "Why are we being punished?"

Double-check

Review

1. Why did both the government and the Communists seek to control Muong Hom?

2. What is a *pho ban?*

3. What does Mr. Petrasy need, to carry out his duties?

4. At what age is a Laotian boy said to become a man?

5. Who are the Khmer Rouge?

Discussion

1. The villagers chose Mr. Petrasy as *pho ban* because of his success as a farmer and his devotion to Buddhism. Do you think these are good criteria on which to base the choice of a leader? On what factors do we base our choices for local leaders in the United States? Are they different from the factors by which the villagers chose Mr. Petrasy? If so, why?

2. How might wars wipe out customs that have been continued for thousands of years? How else might customs with long traditions in a community be wiped out? What, if anything, can or should communities do to preserve their valued customs?

3. How difficult is it to remain neutral in a civil war? What special problems might a person face if he or she were to try to remain neutral? What special problems develop when a person takes sides? Does the proverb Mr. Petrasy quotes sum up the futility — or necessity — of taking sides in a civil war? Explain your answers.

Activities

1. Several students might role-play a reunion of the Petrasy family with Sisouk. Would they trust each other? What would they say about what had happened to them? Other students might role-play a reunion of Ang Eav with her family.

2. A committee of students might hold a panel discussion in front of the class, during which they try to decide what they think will happen in Southeast Asia during the next 10 years.

3. A group of students might plan a three-month trip to Southeast Asia for your class. They could list the cities and other areas they would like to visit, and name the sites, works of art, sporting events, and other things they would like to see, including people they would like to meet.

Skills

MEANWHILE BACK IN THE JUNGLE. . . .

Credit: © United Feature Syndicate

Use the political cartoon above and information in Chapters 18 and 19 to answer the following questions. (Note: Pol Pot forces are the Khmer Rouge.)

1. This cartoon depicts a situation happening in which country?
(a) Laos   (b) Vietnam   (c) Cambodia

2. Why do you think the cartoonist used a frog, a lizard, and a snake to represent the situation?
(a) because they are slimy
(b) to show small animals being swallowed by larger ones
(c) to show national mascots

3. Why did the cartoonist use the term *jungle* here?
(a) It's a hot place.   (b) There are lots of animals.
(c) It is a situation where the strong attack the weak.

4. This cartoon shows that the Vietnamese forces did what?
(a) were defeated by the Pol Pot forces   (b) turned into a snake
(c) defeated the Pol Pot forces

5. How do you think the cartoonist feels about the Pol Pot and Vietnamese forces in Cambodia?
(a) They are equally bad for Cambodia.
(b) They are equally good for Cambodia.
(c) They are both good and bad for Cambodia.

EPILOGUE

NEW CONFLICTS

ALMOST IMMEDIATELY AFTER becoming independent, the majority of the nations in Southeast Asia experienced the pains of growing up and being on their own.

In the three decades after Europeans left, new conflicts arose. The war in Indochina which you read about in Chapters 17, 18, and 19 was the worst of the manmade calamities that visited this part of the world.

However, the Southeast Asian countries outside Indochina had their share of agony during the past three decades. As they moved toward self-government, instability often led to armed conflicts.

Indonesia's Troubles. Indonesia's first president, Sukarno, ruled that island nation for 18 years following independence. He leaned toward the Communist bloc. Communist-inspired student demonstrations shook Jakarta in the early 1960's. An attempted Communist coup in 1965 triggered an anti-Communist backlash. An estimated more than half a million actual or suspected Communists were killed, with an additional one and a half million sympathizers jailed or interned on remote islands.

The anti-Communist general who aborted the Communist uprising, Suharto, eased Sukarno out of power two years later and has since ruled Indonesia.

Indonesia's oil boom in the 1970's helped to bring about economic stability and progress to Indonesia. But in the 1980's, collapsing oil prices threatened economic chaos.

Indonesia's fast growing population—already the fifth-largest in the world—also seriously restrains the economic progress made so far. In the year 2000, it is projected that Indonesia's population will reach 212 million. Its capital city, Jakarta, already estimated to have almost eight million people, will become the 12th most densely populated city in the world with a population of 13.2 million. Over-population is one of the main reasons why few of the benefits of Indonesian's wealth have not reached most of the people.

Still, there is little starvation in Indonesia. The bountiful land and sea around it still provide enough for the people to live on, if not to feast. Outside the cities, Indonesia is a land where people can literally "eat the scenery."

A Broken Federation. Nearby Singapore and Malaysia also went through critical periods of instability after independence. Before his ouster from power, Sukarno opposed the formation of the Federation of Malaysia, which included the island of Singapore. He declared his campaign of *konfrontasi**, or confrontation against the newly-formed federation. Indonesia launched isolated raids and terrorist bombings against Malaysia, but actual war did not break out among the two neighbors.

Within the Federation, clashes between the two largest ethnic groups—Malays and Chinese—caused problems. Singapore is predominantly Chinese, and race riots broke out there in the summer of 1964. By mid-1965, tensions between the two groups were so bitter that Singapore left the Federation to avoid more serious conflicts.

Since their separation, the gap between Malaysian and Singapore has widened. But both countries have tried to live side-by-side peacefully. As neighbors, they want to help each other survive.

Lee Kuan Yew, the first Prime Minister of Singapore after independence, remains the island's undisputed leader. He guided the country through its uncertain and difficult period.

Marcos Ousted. The Philippines went through a bloodless revolution in February 1986. With the help of two military leaders who mutinied against the president, the Filipino people overthrew the 20-year-old regime of President Marcos. Marcos and his family fled into exile in Hawaii.

Marcos was first elected president in 1965, the year most Southeast Asian nations were beginning to manage their own affairs. He was reelected president in 1969. The Philippine Constitution forbid Marcos from serving a third term, but in 1972, a year before the next election, Marcos proclaimed martial law and ruled by decree.

Marcos cited as his major reasons for declaring martial law were the Communist insurgency in the country and the Muslim separatist movement in Mindanao in Southern Philippines.

Some 70,000 people were arrested and imprisoned during Marcos' illegal reign. Among those arrested immediately was Senator Benigno Aquino, Jr. who was regarded by many Filipinos as their most probable next president. Aquino was jailed for eight years and freed in 1980 to undergo a heart bypass operation in the United States.

Aquino returned to Manila on August 21, 1983, and was assassinated upon arrival at the Manila International Airport. Some military men were charged with the murder but were all later acquitted.

The assassination and the acquittal of the accused assassin spurred millions of Filipinos to demonstrate against the Marcos regime in Manila and other Philippine urban centers.

A special presidential election was called by Marcos for February 1986. Aquino's widow, Corazon, became the candidate for the opposition political party. Massive cheating by Marcos and his political party was reported, and Corazon Aquino, supported by a broad section of Philippine society including the religious community, threatened to demonstrate daily until Marcos left. At this point, two military leaders stepped in and supported the people's clamor for change.

President Aquino became the first woman to lead the Philippines and the first woman to lead any nation in Southeast Asia.

The February revolution demonstrated the determination of the Filipino people to make American-style democracy work in the Philippines. They have been trying since they were granted independence in 1946. Under Marcos, the treasury was emptied by corruption and mismanagement.

As the country tried to rebuild itself, Communist insurgency became a serious problem. The Communists exploited agrarian unrest in Central Luzon. Muslims also struggled against Philippine unity. When martial law was imposed in 1972, the Moro National Liberation Front pressed its campaign for a separate Muslim state in Southern Philippines. The Muslim movement died down somewhat, but the Communist insurgents continued to press their campaign despite conciliatory gestures from Aquino.

The United States is particularly concerned over the situation in the Philippines. Its two largest military bases in Asia are located in Central Luzon, and the agreement to keep them there expires before the end of the century.

Burma. On the Asian mainland, in Burma, armed uprisings by Communist factions and Karen tribesmen erupted as soon as the country became independent in 1948. The government won over the rebels by offers of amnesty and giving autonomy to tribesmen.

Socialists took over the Burmese government in the early 1950's and continue to dominate the country. The Communist insurgents now number a few thousands and do not pose a real threat.

Thailand. Also on the Asian mainland, Thailand has been the most tranquil among the Southeast Asian nations since the 1940's. Unlike the other nations of the region which were heavily damaged during World War II, Thailand was spared because it stood practically neutral.

Thailand shares a common border with Cambodia and Laos. In the 1960's it was attacked by Communist guerillas in the north. But true to its tradition of trying to keep out of harm's way, Thailand was careful not to displease the Communist powers on the Asia mainland. In 1975, it established diplomatic ties with the People's Republic of China. And it insisted on the removal of all U.S. military personnel in the country in 1976.

Thai relations with the Vietnamese have not, however, been that stable. This is because refugees have poured into Thailand from Cambodia, Laos, and Vietnam. Vietnamese troops have intruded into Thailand in pursuit of Cambodians resisting Vietnamese occupation of Cambodia.

Many of the conflicts that have affected Southeast Asia in the past decades are part of the struggle to achieve self-government and complete independence. Politically, economically and culturally, Southeast Asia will continue to play an important role in the world. Already, almost 400 million people inhabit the region. At the turn of the century, the region will probably have more than half a billion people.

Pronunciation Guide

The following system translates each syllable into the nearest common English equivalent. Syllables set in capitals are accented. Principal sound equivalents are:

a (as in cat)
ah (as in odd)
ay (as in ale)
ch (as in chair)
e (as in silent)
ee (as in eat)
eh (as in end)
g (as in go)
i (as in charity)
igh (as in ice)
ih (as in ill)
j (as in John)
k (as in keep)
o (as in connect)

oh (as in old)
oo (as in too)
oo (as in foot)
ow (as in out)
s (as in sit)
t (as in tin)
th (as in them)
u (as in cube)
u (as in circus)
uh (unaccented a as in sofa)
ur (as in urn)
y (as in yet)
z (as in zebra)
zh (as in vision)

Abdullah — ahb-DULL-uh
Agung — AH-goong
Anawhrata — ah-NAH-ruh-tuh
Anek Thamthiangsat — ah-NEHK tahm-TEE-ehng-saht
Ang Eav — ahng ave
Angkor — ANG-koor
Annamite — ANN-ah-might
ao dai — ow zye
Ayutthaya — ah-YOO-tah-yuh

Bahasa — buh-HAH-suh
Bangkok — BANG-kahk
barrios — BAHR-ee-ohs
batiks — bah-TEEKS
Batur — bah-TOOR
Bayinnaung — bigh-YIH-nown
Beth Villahermosa — behth VEE-yah-HAYR-moh-suh
Borobudur — bahr-oh-boo-DOOR
bonze — bahnz
Brunei — brew-NIGH
Buddhist — BOO-dihst
buenos días — BWAY-nohs DEE-ahs

Can Tho — kahn toh
Cao Dai — kaow digh
carabao — kare-ah-BAOW
Cebu — say-BOO
Celebes — SEHL-eh-beez
chinlon — CHIN-lon
Chou Ta-Kouan — JOH dah-KWAHN
chula — CHOO-lah
Confucius — kahn-FEW-shus
Constantine Phaulkon — KON-stahn-teen FAHL-kon

Deva Sri — day-wee SHREE
Dien Bien Phu — DEE-ehn BEE-ehn FOO
durian — DUR-ee-an

epow — ee-PAOW

Ferdinand Magellan — FIR-dih-nand ma-JELL-an

gamelan — GAM-uh-lan
Goa — GOH-ah
guerrillas — gah-RILL-uhz
Guinea — GIHN-ee

Hanoi — hah-NOY
harana — hah-RAH-nuh
Himalaya — him-uh-LAY-uh
Hla — h'lah
Ho Chi Minh — ho chee MINN
hpon — h'pon
hua-chiao — huh-wah-jee-ow
Hue — hew-AY
Hung Yen — hung yehn

Indonesia — in-doh-NEE-zhah
Irian Jaya — ERR-ee-uhn JIGH-yuh
Irrawaddy — ee-ruh-WAH-dee

Jakarta — jah-KAHR-tuh
Jalan Petaling — JAH-lahn peh-TAHL-ing

Java — JAHV-ah
Juneau — JOO-noh

Kaaba — KAH-buh
Kachins — KAH-chinz
Kalimantan — kah-lee-MAHN-tahn
Karens — KAH-rainz
kendang — KEHN-dahng
Khmer Rouge — k'mair ruge
Khmers — K'MAIRZ
klongs — klahngz
Koran — KOHR-rahn
Kuala Lumpur — KWAH-lah LUHM-puhr

Laos — LAOW-os
Le Truc Mai — lay trook migh
longyi — LAHN-gee
Luang Prabang — loo-ONG prah-BONG
Luzon — loo-ZON

magandang maga — mah-gahn-DAHNG MAH-guh
Mae Nam Chao Phraya — ma nahm chaow p'hrah-yah
Mah Jongg — mahzh AHNG
mai pen arai — migh pen righ
Majapahit — muh-joh-PAH-heet
Malacca — mah-LAHK-ah
Malaysia — mah-LAY-zhah
Mekong — MAY-kahng
merdeka — mayr-DAY-kuh
Mohammed — moh-HAM-uhd
Molucca — moh-LUCK-ah
Mongkut — MAHNG-koodt
monsoon — mahn-SOON
Muang Thai — MU-wahng TIGH
Muong Hom — mee-AHNG hahm
Mya — mee-AH

Nagas — NAH-guhs
Nanyang — NAHN-yahng
Nawi — NAH-wee
Ngo Dinh Diem — no dinn ZEE-um
nirvana — nur-VAHN-uh

Pagan — pah-GAHN
pandanggo — pahn-DAHNG-goh
Pathet Lao — PAH-tet LAOW
Penang — peh-NAHNG
penchak — pehn-CHAHK
Philippines — fill-ah-PEENZ
Phnom Penh — p'nawm pen

pho ban — foh bahn
Phoune Petrasy — foon peh-trah-SEE
picadillo — pihk-ah-DEE-yoh
Pilipino — pihl-ih-PEE-noh
pirogue — pih-ROHG
puasa — poo-ah-SAH
pwe — pway

Ramadan — RAH-muh-dahn
Rangoon — ran-GOON

Sabah — SAH-bah
sadripu — sah-DREE-pooh
Saigon — sigh-GAWN
Salween — SAHL-ween
San Luis — sahn loo-EES
Sarawak — sah-RAH-wahk
saris — sah-REEZ
sarongs — sah-RAHNGZ
Sepak Raga Jaring — seh-PAHK rah-GUH JAHR-ing
Shans — shahnz
shikkoed — shee-KOH'D
Shwe Dagon — SHWAY duh-GOHN
Siam — sigh-AM
Siddharta Gautama — sih-DAHR-tuh GOH-tuh-muh
Singapore — SING-uh-pohr
sipa — SEE-pah
Sisouk — see-SOOK
Siti — SEE-tee
Sukarno — soo-KAHR-noh
Sulawesi — soo-lah-WAY-zee
Sumatra — sooh-MAH-truh
Sun Yat-sen — soon yaht-sehn
Surabaja — soohr-ah-BAH-yuh

takraw — tahk-RAOW
Tamil — TAM-uhl
Taoism — DOW-ism
Tasaday — TAHS-ah-digh
Thailand — TIGH-land
Timor — TEE-mohr
Tondo — ton-DOH
Tonle Sap — tahn-lee SAHP
towkay — TAOW-kay
Tran Dinh Vien — trahn zinn v'yen

Vasco da Gama — VASS-coh dah GAM-uh
Vientiane — v'yen-T'YAN
Viet Cong — v'yet KONG
Viet Minh — v'yet MINN

Wu Hor Kar — woo hohr kahr

Index

*Photograph.

235